PENGUIN MODERN CLASSICS
Selected Satire

Shrilal Shukla (1925–2011) is one of the most widely read Hindi authors of the twentieth century. His novel *Raag Darbari* won the Sahitya Akademi Award for Hindi in 1969 and became an instant classic. He is recognized broadly as a modern master of Hindi satire.

Matt Reeck has published translations from Hindi, Urdu, and French. His translation from the French of Zahia Rahmani's *Muslim* won the 2020 Albertine Prize. He served as the Princeton University Translator in Residence in 2021.

SHRILAL SHUKLA

Selected Satire
FIFTY YEARS OF IGNORANCE

Translated from the Hindi by Matt Reeck

PENGUIN BOOKS

An imprint of Penguin Random House

PENGUIN BOOKS

USA | Canada | UK | Ireland | Australia
New Zealand | India | South Africa | China

Penguin Books is part of the Penguin Random House group of companies
whose addresses can be found at global.penguinrandomhouse.com

Published by Penguin Random House India Pvt. Ltd
4th Floor, Capital Tower 1, MG Road,
Gurugram 122 002, Haryana, India

Penguin
Random House
India

First published in Penguin Books by Penguin Random House India 2019

ISBN 9780143452195

For Sale in the Indian Subcontinent Only

Typeset in Minion Pro by Manipal Technologies Limited, Manipal

Printed at Thomson Press India Ltd, New Delhi

www.penguin.co.in

MIX
Paper
FSC FSC® C010615

*In honor of the memory of Gerald Reeck (1945–2021),
beloved father, mentor, and friend*

Contents

Translator's Note

In 2017, the Indian government issued a postage stamp to honor the great modern Hindi writer and satirist Shrilal Shukla (1925–2011). No doubt, Shukla would have found humor in this event. There, preserved for eternity (or for however long mail and stamps will last), is his likeness: a clean-shaven elderly man with big round glasses and a wry smile. Perhaps, at the moment the photograph was taken, he was thinking about how his long commitment to literature might be rewarded in the future with a stamp worth ten rupees—or one-third the amount needed to send a domestic letter in India today. Then, from the reader's perspective, the irony of this dubious, posthumous reward also comes from the fact that it was granted by an entity—the Indian government—that was often the object of his satire.

Conversations about Shrilal Shukla likely begin—and just as likely end—with *Raag Darbari* (1968). Shukla's first novel, a satire on small-town society and politics in North

India, won him the Sahitya Akademi Award for Hindi in 1969 and thrust him into the national literary spotlight. The novel remains a critical and popular success. On the fiftieth anniversary of the book's publication, literary critics, social scientists and dramatists from across North India celebrated the occasion with new commentary, productions, and public events.[*] Ravish Kumar, the TV host and managing editor of NDTV, spoke on-air about how the novel continues to describe the everyday world of North Indians. Rajkamal Prakashan, the book's publisher, estimates that more than 500,000 copies have been sold over time, with 25,000 to 30,000 copies selling each year. The book's total readership is thought to be in the tens of millions.[†]

---

[*] Most recently, Mahmood Farooqui and Darain Shahid presented *Dastaan-e-Raag-Darbari*, a retelling of the novel in the style of *dastangoi* narration at the Kamani Auditorium in New Delhi. See Aditi Pancholi, 'A Contemporary Dastaan of Shrilal Shukla's *Raag-Darbari* Regales Delhi Audience', the *Times of India*, 15 January 2020. On 29–30 January 2018, a conference was held at Delhi University convened by Satyajit Singh and entitled 'Polity As Fiction, Fiction As Reality: Fifty Years of *Raag Darbari*'. The conference focused on the intersection of social science and literature, and the novel's lasting value. See Ulka Anjaria, 'Fifty Years Later, Shrilal Shukla's "Raag Darbari" Is Being Reborn As Modern Indian literature', Scroll.in, 3 March 2018.

[†] Ravish Kumar, '"Raag Darbari" Completes 50 Years: A Journey into the Culture of India's Politics', NDTV, 16 March 2018, available at: https://www.youtube.com/watch?v=j-iNgAq83tA. In 2017, the Consortium for Educational Communication in New Delhi produced a video in conjunction with the Swayam.

This volume of selected satire extends conversations about Shukla's work. *Selected Satire: Fifty Years of Ignorance* draws its material from a volume of collected satire that includes some of his most recognized satires outside of *Raag Darbari*.* With 427 pages, *Fifty Years of Ignorance* is a lengthy compilation and the best introduction to Shukla's short satire. This volume of translations provides a broad and representative sample of that book.

Selected Satire: Fifty Years of Ignorance presents Shukla's social, cultural and political short satire. It covers a range of themes, and yet the social, cultural and political dimensions to Shukla's writing intertwine so that assigning a 'type' to any particular essay or story is difficult. Interestingly, the words in both Hindi and Urdu used to designate the general genre in which Shukla's satire would be first categorized—Hindi's 'hasya-vyangya' and Urdu's 'tanz-o-mazah'—do not separate satire from humor writing in general. The phrase 'humor and satire' acknowledges this umbrella genre's internal variety, which is abundantly evident in this volume. Shukla's satire is endlessly rich, with many subject matters, techniques, tones and tropes. By turns critical, sympathetic, sarcastic, honest, self-deprecating, self-satisfied, exaggerated, realistic, ironic and sincere,

Prabha Direct-to-home satellite education project on the novel. See 'Raag Darbari by Shri Lal Shukla (CH_01)', available at: https://www.youtube.com/watch?v=8sDYddihU08. This video represents the second side of Shukla's readership—exam readers.

*   Shrilal Shukla, *Jahaalat ke pachaas saal*, New Delhi: Rajkamal Prakashan, 2004; fifth printing, 2014.

he uses practically all literary genres—stories, but also anecdotes, interviews, closet dramas, aphorisms, literary criticism and poetry—as forms for his humor and critique.[*]

Satire is typically credited with the intention of wanting to effect social change, but I would suggest that we remain skeptical of such claims. Satire, as a skeptical way of looking at the world, asks us to remain as critical of ourselves as of others and as wary of established fact as of uninspected prejudice. The fact that Shukla's satire—some of it written more than a half century ago—continues to accurately describe North Indian life serves as proof that even the best satire cannot by itself change society. Nevertheless, Shukla's keen social observations, literary finesse and abundant humor issue an inviting call for readers to think again not only about the achievements and failures of modern and contemporary Indian society, but also about the strengths and weaknesses of our character in general.

Matt Reeck
August 2021

---

[*]   For a modern history of Hindi satire, please see *Hindi Hasya Vyangya Sankalan*, edited by Shukla and Prem Janmejay, New Delhi: National Book Trust, India, 1997.

1

The Grand Motor Driving School

Above two spare, dirty rooms, there was a sign with big letters announcing 'The Grand Motor Driving School'. On the verandah, a poster listed various activities and their fees, including:

Motor Driving (with license): Rs 3,000
Motor Driving (without license): Rs 2,000

I knew I was in the waiting room because there was a sign reading 'Reception' on top of a rickety table. I asked the receptionist sitting behind the table, 'What does "without license" mean? I have a learner's permit. Does that mean I'll have to pay a thousand rupees more?' The receptionist (who I would learn later was also the cleaning person) was busy using a thin screwdriver to clean his nails. Taking a break from his hygiene routine, he stared at me, then said, 'Other people have asked the same silly question. That's not what Ustad meant on the chart.'

'Then I don't understand.'

'Clearly. Ustad meant that if you only want to learn how to drive, then it's two thousand. But if you want a license too, then it's three.'

'So you make driver's licenses too?'

Someone put a hand on my shoulder. It was Ustad—an elderly man with a salt-and-pepper beard, wearing jeans and a T-shirt. He said to me, 'Come over here, please. I'll explain. The license is made at the regional passport office. But we'll do the work for you. No slap across the face with a sandal, no pushing and shoving, no bribes, no demeaning anything. The license will arrive at your house without any fuss.'

Those days, I was without work. Writers are always unemployed, or, it's due to being unemployed that writers can write. But, in those days, I was *especially* out of work. Doordarshan had hired me to write the script for a serial. It paid pretty well. I got an advance, and the rest would be paid upon the completion of the job. But, in the contract, I didn't see what was written in tiny letters. So, when the job wrapped up, I got only a third of the remaining money. I thought the director had made a mistake. But then I was told that the mistake had been mine. In the contract, it was written that the remaining money would be given to me upon the satisfactory completion of my job. The director told me that the job was completed, but not satisfactorily.

'How's that?' I asked.

The director explained, 'Your script was really excellent. It was just brilliant! First-class! Very impressive! But we want something not as good as that. At best, a second-class or probably third-class script. So, we had to give your script to a run-of-the-mill writer. He had to bring it down a level. Make it mediocre. And we had to pay him a lot to do it.'

As soon as the news about this got out, my stock fell. To get by, I wrote a couple of short stories. But then the Hindi newspapers that had published my stories went out of business. The ones that remained were famous for their light fare, and, to their mind, I was a 'mediocre' writer—me, whose 'brilliant' script had to be given to a real mediocre writer to make it mediocre!

That was when my friend helped me. He told me to go learn how to drive and he would pay the fees. He said, 'There's a lot of retired government workers in your neighborhood. Fate has given them everything except a driver. If you learn how to drive, you can earn enough by driving around a couple retirees. A couple hours of work a day, and you can earn enough. Then you'll be free. Part-time driving and part-time writing! You'll be in heaven.'

I looked into it. I didn't bother looking at the retirees' cars. I looked at the well put-together, well-dressed drivers who drive big-time actors—but, more importantly, actresses—to film sets. At first glance, they seemed less like drivers and more like fans, or sometimes like chatty relatives or silent lovers. Compared to depressed writers criticized for being 'brilliant', I thought this looked like a much more attractive profession.

That day, Ustad spoke to me for an hour about the various parts of a car. His speciality was being able to explain car parts without touching anything. It was an instruction of talking and pointing. Through gestures alone, he taught me how to open a car's hood. When I couldn't open the car hood, he asked the cleaner to do it. Then he explained to me about the carburetor. He said, 'If the car suddenly stops when you're driving, first open the carburetor to take a look to see if gas isn't getting in due to some blockage somewhere.'

I'm among those who haven't gotten married but who are always in wedding parties. It's like I have heard so much about cars that I feel like I know about them. Especially Fiats. Politely opening the door of the Fiat, Ustad, my teacher, acted like I was his teacher.

I repeated to myself, 'If the battery is running low, the car will stop on its own. If you get a flat tire, then . . .'

'Whatever the case,' Ustad interrupted, 'First, you should always check the carburetor. You open it like this . . .'

A little while earlier, I mean, before I got lost in car parts, we had talked about various matters of interest in order to get to know each other, and I had discovered that he was interested in political science. 'The times are bad' . . . 'It's the end of intelligence' . . . 'God is feeding jalebis to his donkeys' . . . 'There's another fool at every turn' . . . he had come up with some original witticisms from his own observations and thinking. So, when he told me that if the car abruptly stopped working, I should check the carburetor first, I replied in a political vein: 'So you're telling me that if we hear that there's a famine in Orissa, we should first check to see if the World Bank is still fulfilling its loan to India or not?'

Ustad smiled for the first time. Then he nodded his head to confirm that he had at last found a worthy student. He said, 'Exactly right! This is exactly what our finance minister is doing.' Then he went back to talking about the carburetor.

A doubt crept into my mind. And it grew larger and larger until I was faced with a new reality. I asked him, 'Do you know Mr Rajat Mittal?'

'Of course. You mean the Director of Mountain Uplift? Why did you think about him right now?'

Three or four years earlier, Mittal Sahib was out on an inspection trip in the mountains. It was a government trip, so it was essential that his children and wife went with him. Suddenly, going up the mountains, the government-issued car stopped. The driver shot out of the car to see what was the matter, and, operating on the principle that you have to first check the carburetor, he opened the hood and started fiddling around. It was another matter that he spared little time to think about whether the hand brake was an important part of the car. He had avoided using it. From the way that he had jostled the stick shift, it was also not clear just which gear the car was in.

'I thought of it, Ustad,' I said, 'because when his driver got out to check the carburetor, the car started slipping down the hill and . . .'

Ustad laughed, 'I know the whole story. The driver was my nephew. I'm the one who taught him how to drive.'

I should have been upset on Mittal Sahib's behalf. I said angrily, 'That idiot was taking Mittal Sahib and his children's lives into his own hands! They were lucky to escape only with broken bones!'

There was no remorse or sadness in Ustad's voice. It was as if he had come from a dip in the holy water at

Geeta Kund. He said, 'But it was really about the stick shift, wasn't it? The driver didn't put it in gear properly. It was in neutral. The car started to slip down the slope. Everyone jumped out of the car. They got a couple broken arms and legs. But ask yourself this—did anyone ever find out if the carburetor *wasn't* the problem?'

What could I say to that? To keep the conversation going, I said, 'What's your nephew doing these days?'

'Mittal Sahib fired him. Right now the Supreme Court is hearing their case. In the meantime, he's driving a private bus.'

'In the mountains?'

'Yes, just like before.'

There are holy men who run organizations that make millions of rupees but who never touch money themselves. Ustad was a little like them. He ran a driving school but never touched a car. If you told him to touch the head of a black cobra, he would, but he would never touch a steering wheel. It was the cleaner's job to teach people how to hold the steering wheel, as long as he wasn't busy being the receptionist.

Two weeks of instruction passed. I was gradually learning how to drive. The cleaner was back at the reception desk, and when I took the Fiat out to drive, Ustad was with me.

Barbers—whom everyone now calls hair dressers, and whose specialties now include (due to popular demand) the tasks of dentists—tell such wonderful stories that their customers forget that there's a pair of scissors or a razor blade working its way around their heads, or a file or drill inside their mouths. They forget the potential dangers of sharp razors for the head and hellish drills for the mouth! Ustad too could talk on and on without interruption about anything in the world, including driving, which was not part of my narrow experience at all. And that's what he was doing.

He was talking about accidents. He was recounting glorious stories about drivers back when cars were new, back when drivers were respected like airplane pilots are today. Ustad didn't place any importance in accidents. 'Even good horsemen fall in the course of battle,' he said.

'But, Ustad,' I shot back, 'you can't say that about driving a car. If you're riding a horse, the worst that will happen is that the horse will throw you. But with driving, it's not just about the driver and the car. You can also crash into a handful of innocent people innocently walking down the road. If you fall off a horse, no problem. Just stay on the ground. But if a car runs someone over, then that's it for you! If you escape the crowd that comes to beat you up, then you won't escape the gates of the jail shutting behind you!'

'Okay, but you're just used to seeing the worst in everything.'

These words struck home. And suddenly I heard the sound of the left side of the Fiat scraping against the side of a truck parked along the road. 'Let's stop and check to see if the damage isn't too bad,' I said.

'The insurance agents will tend to it. Keep going.'

The street was clear up ahead. Ustad continued to talk about accidents, 'Don't worry about accidents. Actually, the word is nonsense. What happens is an "incident". And what happened? That which always happens.'

'Ustad, this is a complicated philosophy.'

'If Indians become modern only by renouncing philosophy, then what use is Indianness to us?' He fell silent for a moment, then started talking again, 'You were just asking about someone being run over by a car and dying. In these instances, sometimes it's not bad for the driver, but rather, how should I put it? Here's a story about how it can be lucky for a driver. But it's not a story, it's actually true. It happened to my nephew.'

'The mountain uplift one?'

'No, another one. The plains uplift one.'

But was it uplift or sinkhole? The accident—or the incident—went along these lines: The nephew was driving an Ambassador at 100 kilometres per hour. It was on a state highway. The highway was empty. It was eleven at night. In the car, it was just the nephew in the front and the groggy government official in the back. The nephew wasn't sleepy at all. He was alert for five reasons: he was young; it was a new car; it was a great road; he had drunk some moonshine; and, at the end of the trip, a prostitute was waiting for him. The flickering lights of clay lamps and the dim gleam of village (and bigger village) light bulbs dotted the night like specks on a dark canvas. The car was going fast. Life goes by fast, and death comes quickly. Perhaps that was the point that the bicyclist meant to prove when he suddenly exited an alley going full speed and without checking to see what might be coming down the road.

The bicycle hit the car, was spun around several times, then landed with a ferocious crash alongside the road.

And the cyclist? He didn't fall, but he sprang into the sky. He landed on the car's hood, then windshield. His body spread out over the hood, broke the windshield and then came to a rest on the seat to the left of the driver. The passenger's seat was soaked in blood, and there was a monstrous, bloody face looking down, like it was inspecting the scene. The driver lost control of the wheel. The mangled car skidded off the road. There were no irrigation ditches along the road, only rough land and dry fields. The car hit a fence and stopped. Thank goodness it was only the driver's hand that slipped from the wheel, and that his foot was still hovering just over the brake pedal as was his habit!

The highway had been empty, but now there was a crowd of villagers. And suddenly it was loud and chaotic. Collapsed half-dead on the backseat, the official in the backseat was screaming. The driver didn't think it possible to flee the scene so he curled up into the fetal position and started mumbling gibberish, something to the effect that it wasn't his fault. Suddenly, two policemen emerged from out of the crowd, and they took the driver and the official to the police station. The crowd followed. The station was no more than half a kilometre away.

At the station, the official was given a chair. He sat down, reached into his pocket, then cast a questioning glance at the officer at the station's front desk. The answer he got was that there was no chance of bribery here. The clerk said, 'Wait till Daroghaji arrives.' The surprising thing was that the driver wasn't locked up. He was sitting outside on a bench.

When the darogha arrived, he went outside to talk to the villagers. Then a dozen or so men were loaded into a jeep and taken to the scene of the accident, or incident. There, police had been keeping watch over the dead man stuck in the windshield, and over the car stuck in the field. In the middle of the wild shouting at the scene, the darogha inspected the corpse with great discipline. Then he said, 'This is him.' The silence of the night was drowned in the villagers' cries of 'Victory! Victory!' Some motioned to the heavens in thanks, and some fired their double-barreled shotguns into the air in celebration.

In the early morning, when a bus stopped to take the chief officer, the official and the driver back to the city, the latter two men had garlands around their necks as they boarded the bus.

Cries of 'Long live X! Long live Y!' filled the air.

There had been a bloody murderer in the area. The government had posted a wanted poster, promising 20,000 rupees to whomever captured him, dead or alive. He had already shot several police officers in stand-offs. The police had been looking for him for ages.

The man who had committed suicide—and who was now hanging through the windshield of the Ambassador— was that very criminal. The official was smiling. The driver was pretending to be in the know, so he wasn't smiling. But he knew in his heart of hearts that while Daroghaji would confiscate much of the reward, there would still be a couple of thousand rupees for him.

There are no accidents in this world, only incidents. Some are good; some aren't so good. This was Ustad's philosophy.

The next day, I didn't get a lesson on philosophy, but one on political science and sociology. It was my final day of class. After that, I would sit at home, keeping all of my dignity, and wait for the driver's license to arrive in a dignified manner, for 1000 rupees, without having to pay any bribes to middlemen. As I took the car out onto the road, it would be the last time I would sit as a driver-in-training next to Ustad.

It was five in the evening. The road led out of town, and people were leaving their offices to drive home. I was nervous.

Ustad was explaining one of the finer points of philosophy in the voice of a dental surgeon trying to put the patient to sleep. I gazed ahead and anxiously drove the Fiat down the street.

Suddenly, at a distance, a police officer gestured for me to stop. And that was my undoing. Confused, I hit the gas pedal instead of the brake. Instead of stopping, the car sprang forward like a deer, and, by the time I could find the brake, the car had already bashed into the rear end of a parked car and jerked to a stop. The 'incident' didn't matter to Ustad. But I started to bleed from my nose. Drops of blood fell onto my shirt. The police officer ran up to us. Not listening at all to the officer's curses, Ustad turned to me and said, 'Don't worry. I have a good remedy for nosebleeds.'

. Then, police officers surrounded us. One officer was wearing white pants and a bush shirt. I was told that the large car that I had struck was that of an officer at the Regional Transport Office. He was the man in the white pants. The other cops were his men. They were on duty making car stops, checking for licenses.

I showed them my learner's permit, and their anger subsided. They began to be interested in my bloody nose. Suddenly, the officer asked Ustad for his license. Without hesitation, Ustad answered, 'I don't drive, so why would I have a license?'

The officer looked at the advertising on the car—'The Grand Motor Driving School'. He asked, 'Who runs this school?'

'I do.'

'Who sits next to the students to teach them how to drive?'

'I do.'

'But you don't have a license?'

'No.'

'So how can you teach someone to drive?'

Ustad took pity on the RTO officer. And, as though he were speaking to a moronic kid, he said, 'These are two different things, sir. Driving a car is one thing, but teaching driving is another. You're the expert in the first case, and I'm the expert in the second case.'

The RTO officer was confused. He said sharply, 'In my opinion, before teaching others to drive, you should be able to prove that you can drive. And how can you do that without a license? I'm going to give you a ticket.'

'Go ahead, but how can you prove that I know how to drive?'

This puzzled the officer. He thought about Ustad's question for a minute, then started laughing—Ha! Ha! Ha! Ha! Ha! Ha! Ha! Ha! Ha!

I couldn't believe that the sound he emitted was really laughter.

Getting a hold on himself, the RTO officer addressed us in a way appropriate for his office. 'You mean that without the foggiest notion of how to drive yourself, you're teaching others to drive?'

'Exactly, sir. Exactly correct!' Ustad leaned his left elbow onto the RTO car's hood, and, as though he were addressing the gathered masses in front of the Red Fort, he said, 'But why is this so surprising? This is exactly what's going on everywhere in the country. Take yourself for example. You're an MA in Sanskrit, but you're working at the RTO. I know a millionaire suffering from a venereal disease. That VD is all he knows about medicine, but now he's running a private medical college. I know another man who was a guard at a road tollbooth. His entire life experience was limited to lowering the barrier to make the oncoming car stop. And now he's the Home Minister in some state, teaching police captains how to get around the law! These days, having been a herder of water buffalos is a qualification for chief minister, and, as soon as "bhak bhak" comes out of your mouth, it instantly becomes policy! Yet, the chief minister is confident—over-confident, even—that if you can herd water buffalos, then you can run a state of a hundred million people. Because, in the first case, it's water buffalos, and, in the second case, it's sheep. You must know the story of the man who couldn't even find his way to a seat on the district council, and then, suddenly, he was the prime minister? So, why are you asking to see my driver's license? Go anywhere from here to Delhi and check all the politicians, none is much better than me. But if you want to give me a fine, go ahead. Just don't complain later that I didn't tell you everything. I mean, I'm an exception. The normal rules don't count for me. I'm not one of the masses. I'm a VIP. As it happens, your transport minister is my nephew."

Ustad then looked at me, and, seeing my questioning glance, he said, 'Yes, my third nephew. But he was never a driver. At first, he was a bus conductor, but when he got caught up in union activities, he had to wash his hands of that. Then he got desperate, and now, the poor guy, he's a minister.'

2

Dogs and More Dogs

These days there are a lot of books written in Indian English that have to do with dogs—real dogs—*Dog Care by a Dog Lover, German Shepherd Dogs by a Dog Lover, Of Dogs and Bitches by a Dog Lover* and so on.

The dog lover's name was G. Prasad or Ghirrau Prasad. He was a straightforward, honest man. He woke up on time and went to bed on time. He laughed at the appropriate moments and cried at the appropriate time. He never ate meat, and he never drank liquor. He prayed for two hours a day, and he kept an astrologer at home. For two or three months a year, he also lodged a wandering saint. In order to be modern, he had an English-speaking wife, he knew a good tailor, he wore thick glasses and he had hemorrhoids.

I don't know how it all came to pass. He was a high-ranking income tax officer. Along with this, or before all else (or from a historical perspective, after all was said and done), he was a dog specialist.

His old friends know that ten years ago his only topics of conversation were his office and his father-in-law—a top official in the railway who spent most of his time telling people off. 'You don't know Daddy,' the son-in-law would say, 'he really told off the Railway Board!'

But then suddenly he started talking about dogs. Overnight he became a dog lover.

The story started something like this.

A neighbor's dog started coming over to his house. At first glance, the dog looked quite loveable. There was no telling why the neighbor had renounced ownership over it. But, like many newly liberated countries, the dog found its situation getting worse and worse. His foot was lame, and this was proof of his deteriorating condition. More than that, the dog's body became covered in dark spots, either from keeping bad company or from want of food. If the dog had been a developing country, these were the type of spots that would have made it possible to invoke the spirit of international cooperation to ask for donations of wheat. But a dog can't whimper its way into becoming a country, just as a country can't become a dog through wretchedness and whining. In the end, this dog wandered over from the neighbor's to Mr G. Prasad's bungalow, and, in spite of whimpering continuously and spinning in circles on his lawn like a plague-stricken rat, the dog couldn't get even a bit of bread from the soon-to-be dog lover. A mountain of unfamiliarity stood between the dog and Mr Prasad. A river of contempt separated them, the sort of contempt that can become the source of international tension between developing and developed countries.

Gradually, the dog's spots grew more numerous, his fur started to fall out and his lameness grew more severe. Even then, Mr G. Prasad wouldn't pay the dog any attention.

But then, one day, a young businessman made a tunnel in the mountain of estrangement separating the dog and Mr Prasad.

This young businessman was, like his father, a lounger on cushions, a worshipper of Lakshmiji, a wearer of a folded, fancy turban, a worshipper of cows and a drinker of bhang lassis. But then he modernized, and so he no longer had to worry about washing after touching someone's pet dog. At his office, tables, chairs, glass walls and an intercom had already made their appearance; and he knew that at home he wouldn't be considered a modern man until he started talking about the horticultural projects of his colleagues, the qawwali he heard the night before at the club, the English poetry of Baba and Baby, the cures for constipation, the strategies for Indian rummy and flush, the whiskey he bought for cheap through the army, how 'the times are bad' and 'honesty is dead' and the pet dogs and cats at home.

So, when Mr Prasad went out to the lawn to meet this young businessman, he found the latter petting the dog. When they greeted each other and exchanged the mandatory 'the times are so bad' and 'honesty is dead' mantras, and after the two were seated in lawn chairs, the young businessman stopped what he was saying, stroked the dog again and said, 'This dog is a pure bred.'

Mr Prasad looked closely at the dog for the first time, and he was appalled. He said that Daddy—his father-in-law—had kept so many dogs and puppies that he had had to put up a 'BEWARE OF DOG' sign on his bungalow. Snapping his fingers, the young businessman continued to play with the dog. But the dog rejected taking advantage of this encouragement.

Finally, the young businessman said that the dog was sick, that it must be taken to the hospital and, if Mr Prasad had no objection, then he would put the dog in his car and take him to Dr Hafiz, the current expert in the city on dog illnesses, and to whom Mr Tandon, Mr Shukla, Mr Vedi, Mr Dwivedi, Mr Trivedi and Mr Chaturvedi all take their dogs.

Mr Prasad put on an actor's voice to say that Daddy's dogs were very strong. They never got sick. Then the truth spilled out. He said coarsely, 'If you want the dog, it's yours to love. It's not mine.'

A gambler learns to control their facial tics. It wasn't what the businessman was expecting, but, like before, he said energetically that the dog lived in Mr Prasad's bungalow, so whether it was his or not, it would have to keep up this lifestyle.

So the dog's medical treatment began in earnest. Under treatment, the dog started to spring to life, just like a developing country. When people came by, they started to remark upon how good the dog looked. And so, after a little while, Mr Prasad adopted the dog, and his kids started playing with it, and all the businessmen agreed that once the ritual 'times are bad' and 'honesty is dead' mantras were invoked, and just so long as Daddy's name wasn't mentioned, then dogs too were a possible topic of conversation.

But, one day, Mr Prasad's dog was run over by a businessman's car. This man's business was well established, but he wasn't rich. Not being rich, he bought vulgar photographs and bad records, he wore clothes that were more ostentatious than necessary, he called politicians and important officials by their first names even though he wasn't their friend, he played bridge every day without really knowing the rules, he drank too much despite getting drunk easily and he drove a car even though he didn't know how to drive. So, when he backed up to leave Mr Prasad's, the dog got caught underneath the car, and thus it was dispatched at once to the proverbial 'happy hunting grounds'.

It was natural for Mr Prasad to be sad. And for the businessman too. It was also natural for the businessman to think that no wrong couldn't be made right. So, he bought a dog just like the dead one, only more expensive, and presented it to Mr Prasad as an act of contrition and compensation. Mr Prasad granted that this was the act of a good man.

The business community soon learned of the accident. Another businessman came to the house, saying that his bitch had had some puppies of such-n-such breed and would Mr Prasad like to have one? Then another came with another puppy of another breed. And the scenario repeated again, again and again. In the end, all the businessmen presented one or two puppies of whichever breeds, and Mr Prasad accepted them with his natural noble spirit.

When we receive gifts, our passion for giving grows. So, after he had been given more than a dozen dogs, he started divvying them up among his friends, especially his friends in other cities. He called them on the phone long distance. He told them that he had got such-n-such sort of dog that he could send on, if his friend liked. And so, Mr Prasad's dog export business grew, and his fame as a dog lover grew. From time to time, a friend of a friend of Mr Prasad would say that his kids were after him for a Pekinese. Mr Prasad's friend would reply that he would call Mr Prasad long distance. Then Mr Prasad would ask a businessman with a Pekinese that had babies every other month if he could spare two puppies, and the puppies would be sent straight away to his friend's house.

Slowly, a love for reading up on dogs grew, and, one day, a popular bookseller came to the house, and Mr Prasad snatched up a dozen or so titles about dogs. A second bookseller noticed some gaps in Mr Prasad's collection and gave him another twenty odd books. A third ordered a handful of dog-related Western magazines. The owner of a photography store gave him a bunch of dog photographs, and, in the end, a publisher brought together all these efforts with a final coordination effort—or 'coordination and dovetailing' in bureaucratese. The publisher happened to notice (and in the exact ratio to which he found himself in hot water over his taxes) that the nation lacked books on dogs. He suggested that Mr Prasad write a couple of books about dogs and send them his way, and, thus, one of the nation's most glaring lacunas would be filled.

But Mr Prasad objected. He said that, as a government worker, a religious man, a householder and a follower of astrology and Swami Satyanand, he was too busy. And

Daddy, too, was about to come on a long vacation. But the publisher insisted. He said that colonial British officers had written thousands of books on Indian birds and flora. He reassured Mr Prasad that his English was of the highest quality and that all he would need was a stenographer, and, moreover, Miss Lily, who just two years before had been chosen as Ms Mussoorie, worked for them, and he was willing to send her over for the task at hand. But Mr Prasad kept saying that he didn't have any free time. Then the publisher said that, in addition to the stenographer, he would get help for Mr Prasad from a college lecturer, a man who wrote textbooks under the title of 'a college graduate'. This man could actually write the 'dog lover' series for Mr Prasad. He forced him to say 'yes', and so the book—*Of Dogs and Bitches by a Dog Lover*—came onto the market.

Mr Prasad's career then took off. Up till then, he had never given a speech that was not in conjunction with his government job. For this, he couldn't press Miss Lily and the 'graduate' into service. But, suddenly—this is what we call a miracle—he started talking extemporaneously. What happened was his neighbor insulted him. His neighbor was a high-ranking official with the railways. Because Mr Prasad was related to Daddy, this neighbor used to come over quite a bit. His neighbor raised cats. He had already made fun of Mr Prasad for his dogs.

One day at the club, conversation turned to cats and dogs, as Mr Prasad sipped a Coca-Cola, and his neighbor, a whiskey. His neighbor attacked Mr Prasad straight away, saying that those who raised dogs soon became dogs themselves, and that if there was anything loveable on earth, it was cats.

By that time, Mr Prasad had begun to love dogs through and through. He picked up a chair in anger. He knew as much about his neighbor as any wise man should. Using this information to its fullest effect, he addressed his neighbor with respect, since he was the same age as Mr Prasad's father-in-law. 'Sir, we're not really talking about cats and dogs, but principles. Please look at the principles at stake. What motivations are operating behind our interests, I mean, hobbies? Usually, we take an interest in things in our orbit and with which we have continuous contact. We should learn from this lesson about how our interests grow. You must have noticed in developed countries how, beyond staple goods, luxury items begin to be produced in just this fashion. Why do we have so many cameras, transistor radios, tape recorders and refrigerators? Because, in the beginning, some people from here went to Europe or America or Japan, and they got these things for free, or for cheap. That's how we started to have an interest in these things—by being around them.'

Suddenly, he noticed that people were listening with rapt attention. He was giving a speech. He hesitated, but then he gathered his courage and continued, 'This theory is applicable to dogs and cats. It was a coincidence that one day a dog came to my house and that Mr Horton gave you all his cats before leaving for England. Please don't forget that these cats could have come to my house, and that the dog could have gone to yours. That's why we shouldn't talk about dogs and cats. It's really about habits. That's what the theory of the development of hobbies is about, and . . .'

His neighbor thought that perhaps Mr Prasad had become drunk on Coca-Cola. But, the very next day, Mr Prasad was invited to give a lecture at the Rotary Club on dog care. His expertise on dogs was accepted to be among the best that anyone knew. He began to be invited to inaugurate dog shows, and his wife, to give out the awards. Wherever he was transferred, a Dog Welfare Association was founded under his leadership. After experiencing these levels of success, eventually, he had the spiritual realization that his life too had a meaning, and it was dogs.

3

The Poetry Festival of Ghursari

The people of the village of Ghursari had to travel sixteen miles to see dust kicked up by a freight truck, thirty-two miles to see smoke rising from a train engine and sixty-four miles to reach the district court. The few times that the mailman had cause to visit, it was like Vasco da Gama had come. If the police chief appeared in the vicinity, for two or three miles in any direction, the news spread that Christopher Columbus was on his way.

One day, it happened that the village's leading politician, Ballamter Maharaj, became a member of the district commission. No one had come forward to contest his candidacy. Everyone said that that would have been disrespectful. In the end, he was elected without a challenger. And then many more things happened without challenge, as well. An elementary school opened, although boys from middle school also studied there. When the school changed into a middle school, high school boys also studied there. When it became a high school, everyone went ahead and called it a college and so it became famous far and wide. To connect the 'college' to a paved road, a sixteen-mile-long dirt road was constructed, and this road managed to cut right through the fields of Ballamter Maharaj's dire enemies. So, where ox-drawn carts had plied from time immemorial, well, there they remained. And where there had been open sewers in times gone by, they were still there in the present day. And where the road cut through the fields, the fields spread back over the road. But the village became a village with a road.

Pandit Dasadin Sharma, Ballamter Maharaj's nephew, became the principal of the college. When it had been a middle school, he was its headmaster. When it had been a high school, he was its only graduate. Now that it was a college, he finally got his BA. Like Akbar, he controlled the college through wiles alone, and, for this, he was famous throughout the world!

At the college, Babu Ramadhar, penname Pallauji, was appointed the Hindi teacher. He had an MA in Hindi. And thus he was a poet. And thus he was always under the impression that others wanted to hear him recite poetry. And thus people were wary of him. And so he lived alone. And so in these conditions, he wrote more poetry and wanted to recite it. And so people grew even more distrustful. And so the cycle remained unbroken.

In the midst of this, two orders came from the college board of directors. One, Dasadin Sharma had to undergo some training, or else he couldn't continue to be principal. Two, the college's illegal additions had to be demolished. Pandit Dasadin set about solving these matters himself.

He told Pallauji that the superintendent was a poetry buff. Hearing this, Pallauji let his imagination bloom like a flower! Posters were printed announcing the school's yearly festival—which would include track and field events, a wrestling competition, word games, one-act plays and an all-India poetry festival—and that the Master of Ceremonies would be none other than the famous scholar, Sir Janardandas, MA, Superintendent of the College.

And the festival was a raging success. From the tug-of-war between the teachers and the students to the principal's speech, from the exciting wrestling matches to the distribution of prizes by Ballamter Maharaj—all was jubilation. The only hiccup occurred during the last night's one-act plays. In playing the role of a ticket collector, one very clever student actor carried on in such a side-splitting manner that the audience fell over laughing. When the boy left the stage, the crowd kept calling for him to come back. Pandit Dasadin Sharma gave him four lashes for indecent language. Nevertheless, the performance was a big success, and the crowd left saying how great the ticket collector had been and how they'd never seen anything so good. Now all that remained was the final event—the all-India poetry festival.

The festival provided Pallauji with a new excuse to indulge in poetry, and so he left no stone unturned in putting together a hit line-up. He sent the schoolboys out to far-flung locales, he combed the vicinity for anyone he knew, he asked poets to invite their friends and he seemed bent on spreading the good word of literature into the most remote and backward regions. Singing at full tilt the mantra of 'Hindi! Hindu! Hindustan!' he received, in the end, the acceptance notes of several good Hindi poets.

Ballamter's younger brother Ramanjore took responsibility for the poets' lodging. Ramanjore was already familiar with this type of work, for, in the village, he alone was responsible for puppet shows, nautanki plays and Ramlila re-enactments. Ramanjore wore a red shawl over his shoulders and dots of lime slake on his ears. He wore a T-shirt; a long bandana was cinched around his waist and a gold amulet was hanging from his neck. He was chewing bhang, and tobacco flakes dotted his lower lip and teeth. His palms were also stained from tobacco. When you saw Ramanjore, you believed he could get anything done. So, when he spat out his tobacco very close to Pallauji's feet and said quite without concern, 'Everything will work out. Pallauji, what are you mumbling about?' Pallauji realized that he needn't say anything more.

Ramanjore called the farmers back from the fields and set them to prepare the lodging for the poets. There was a bungalow-like barn with a thatched roof where the farmers kept their cows and water buffalos. The men herded these animals out and tied them near the base of the banyan tree. Whinnying, neighing and voicing their protest, the horses and foals too were led out of the barn and were tied up. Immediately, they started to pull up the stakes where they were tied. Inside the barn, the animal piss and poop was cleaned up, ash was spread then swept up, then leaves and heaps of straw were laid down. School mats were laid down on top of this. On three sides of the barn, there were troughs a foot or so off the ground that were usually used for livestock feed. Water smelling of a mixture of old straw, grain, cottonseed oil cakes and salt was drained from the troughs and flung out the back of the barn. The troughs were cleaned and wiped dry, then filled with dry straw. In one corner, two new troughs were placed. Ramanjore instructed the workers to fill one with clay mugs and leaf plates, and the other with drinking water, so that these things would always be on hand. Ramanjore scanned the scene with the glance of a lax supervisor, then picked up his long bandana and rushed to one corner of the barn. In an athletic show of strength, he lifted the thatched roof. It took a lot of effort; to show this, Ramanjore grit his teeth. And yet he was very strong; to show this, he puffed out his chest as he propped the thatched roof up with two bamboo poles. Then he blew out all the pent-up air in his lungs and said, 'Call Pallauji. He should see how I've turned this place into a palace.'

At the end of the afternoon, Ujagar Sharma was called from the neighboring village to take up residence in the barn, now called a 'community centre'. He was known for singing the stories of Radheshyam Kathavachak while playing the harmonium. Within minutes, Kodairam Brahmbhatt also appeared. He was dressed in a dhoti raised to his knees, a mirjai cotton jacket, a safa turban and he sported an impressive moustache. Seeing him, Ujagar Sharma laughed, 'Pallauji's really done it!' Kodairam answered tersely, 'Give it a rest. He's one great schemer.'

As the evening drew on, two ox-drawn carts pulled into Ghursari stuffed with city poets. Approaching the village, the oxen started to run with heavy footfalls. By the sound of bells clanking and clonking from the necks of the oxen, the sound of the cart drivers calling out 'ban-ban kan-kan' and the rattling and shaking of the wheels, everyone knew that the poets had arrived. The high-school boys started up their band. The elementary-school boys stood in rows and played a noisy folk tune with bells. The foals bucked and bucked, breaking free from their stakes. Each mare grabbed the tail of its foal and, together, they raced out of town. One or two farmers sprinted for the community centre. Ramanjore sat on the roots of the banyan tree. He stood up and in a loud voice shouted, 'Hey, Pallauji! Guests have arrived!'

The faces of the poets were covered in dust. As soon as the poets descended from the cart, they started beating the dust off their clothes. Duffle bags, briefcases, blankets and sacks were handed down. One farmer started throwing the luggage into the community centre as though it was a bunch of gunnysacks filled with sorghum. All the unemployed and shiftless souls of the village gathered to watch. The boys surrounded the door to the community centre. They ate raw chickpeas, sucked on sticks of sugarcane and played slap tag. Their hair drenched with castor oil, their parts marked with vermillion paste, their eyes lined with kohl, some very black women wearing very black dhotis sat on their haunches and gossiped. Ramanjore looked over everything like an expert, then aggressively yelled at the crowd, 'Out! Everyone out! Or else I'll snap your legs in two!' Now the poets were forced to look at him. Pallauji introduced Ramanjore to them. Tying his bandana firmly around his waist, he stepped forward in the manner of a bodybuilder. When he reached the poets, he greeted them with two-handed handshakes.

Sugarcane juice was warmed, then milk was added, and this drink, along with a special pea dish, was served to the poets as a snack. Two village barbers with their little brass pots were brought to sit on top of the well, and the poets were informed that they could now freshen up.

When it was time for dinner, leaf plates were taken from one trough, and clay mugs were taken from the other, then filled with drinking water. Then, suddenly, there was a great ruckus in the kitchen, and it was clear that food was on the way. A half-dozen or so muscular young men with dhotis raised to their knees, their holy lock waving back and forth on their shaved heads and their sacred threads wrapped around their bare trunks emerged from the kitchen alongside Ramanjore. They brought the food out, then started frantically serving. When one said 'Rice!', the cry of 'rice' echoed through the community centre then back to the kitchen. Another said, 'Yogurt's out!' and the cry of 'yogurt, yogurt' reverberated through the countryside for 150 miles!

The meals were served: two dollops of yogurt (the servers scooped the yogurt out of pots with their fingers), lentils and a fistful of rice. Now the poets started looking at one another. One poet asked Ramanjore, 'If you don't mind—what's his name?—Pallauji—could you please ask him to come?'

Leaning against the trough filled with straw, Ramanjore watched the proceedings. He called out weakly for Pallauji, then went up to the poet in question, gingerly sat down and asked him kindly, 'What happened? What's wrong?'

The poet said something in English to a female poet seated not too far away, then said to Ramanjore, 'Sheilaji and I can't eat this type of food.'

Ramanjore burst out laughing. He said, 'Okay, then, if you insist! No problem. If you don't want country organic, we can make you some deep-fried city food.' Then he spoke to one of the muscular young servers, 'Over here! We need some puri! On the double!' Followed by, 'And make it quick, or else!'

The poets couldn't believe it. The complaining poet had some harsh words in English for Ramanjore. Then the female poet added some more. Another poet pointed to the water trough. A fourth took a piece of dried cow dung from underneath a school mat and threw it at Pallauji. A fifth poet, not being able to single out anything in particular, simply started cursing. In this state of affairs, the revivalist of Kathavachak shouted out to Kodairam. The two spoke briefly. Then Kodairam put on his performance face, cleared his throat and started slowly singing, 'D—d—dd—ur—ur—ur—urga . . .' It was the first line of a six-line chappay stanza. Then Ramanjore saw Pallauji coming from the kitchen. He bellowed, 'What's wrong, Pallauji? Why are you worried?' Then, from all four directions, the strong young servers suddenly descended, repeating, 'What's wrong?' By the time they got to the poets, the young men looked quite cross. The poets fell silent. Some started eating, while others said they were waiting for the puri.

Then someone said something to Ramanjore. He repeated it to Pallauji. Pallauji repeated it to the poets. Then Pallauji shouted in every direction, 'Ballabhji is here! Ballabhji is here!' In the very next instant, the poet Ballabhji entered the community centre. One poet cursed at him, then turned to his neighbor and said, 'Last year, I invited him to my festival. He wanted hundreds of rupees. And now, for four sorry rupees, he's willing to bicycle sixteen miles?' Another poet offered a seat to Ballabhji and, with great affection said, 'In this dark, and this cold, and on a bike—it's really too much!' Ballabhji sat down with a thump. He spoke slowly, 'This place isn't easy to find. Maheshji wrote me a note, and so I came. I couldn't refuse Maheshji.'

The poets spared nothing in their critique of the festival's lackluster arrangements. They cursed out the organizer. Yet, when Ballabhji, the Cyclist, mentioned Maheshji, it was as though he reminded the poets of a forgotten mantra. One poet said to the next, 'I would never, ever have come. But Maheshji wrote. I came because I love him so much.' The interlocutor replied, 'The same for me! Maheshji's letter forced my hand.' Another poet asked a colleague, 'You were going to Delhi?' The answer came, 'Well, what could I do? Maheshji told me to come.' Another asked, 'How did you get time off from work?' Another answered, 'Who said anything about time off? But I couldn't refuse Maheshji.' Someone asked softly, 'How much did it cost to get here?' Someone answered obstreperously, 'Why are you asking about the fare? I came out of love for Maheshji! I would have paid anything!' Now all these poets, embarrassed about having come to Ghursari, muttered Maheshji's name for cover. They started laughing and talking among themselves. Pallauji stroked his chin in contemplation and wondered who this Maheshji really was.

The poetry festival started around ten at night. The previous day, the ticket collector had earned high marks for his acting, and now the same space was set up for poets. Behind the stage was a screen on which Shivaji, wielding a sword, sat on a horse. To each side, there were images of fairies bathing in ponds. The Chairman and the poets were seated on stage. There was a party tent set up in front of the stage where three or four hundred people were seated. Beyond the tent in every direction, four to five thousand people were seated in the dew. A little way away, beneath a tree near the gate, several watchmen were warming themselves around a bonfire. Some police officers were lying on charpoys and smoking bidis. A boy performed a nautanki routine. The cries of vendors selling peanuts, amaranth laddoos and sesame brittle resounded in the smoky light from country lanterns. Seeing this, MC Janardandas puffed out his neck like a pigeon and called out to Pallauji, 'Please make them stop. Let's begin the recitation.' Pallauji passed the news on to Ramanjore. Ramanjore stomped off the stage and went up to the police officers, 'Divanji, it's about to start. Please get the nautanki to stop.' Then he went up to the hawkers and yelled at them, 'Sit down and shut up, you bastards. Or I'll tear off your legs.' With this, silence descended.

First, Pandit Dasadin Sharma gave a speech, the gist of which was that no one knew how to write Hindi poetry any longer. Pallauji's speech followed, in which he professed that *some* poets could write Hindi poetry, and these few souls were all gathered that night in Ghursari. Then the recitations began. First, Ujagar Sharma sang a prayerful quatrain from his Radheshyam Kathavachak repertoire. Then the female poet, who came from the city, sang a love poem. In the course of singing, she looked out at the crowd and grew nervous. There were around 4000 people sitting there, with their scarves wrapped around their heads to protect them from the cold, and holding clubs and sticks that seemed to reach to the sky. Everyone was smoking bidis or marijuana chillum pipes. It was almost completely silent, and, in that silence, the female poet could only think of the badlands along country rivers and of Sultana Daku, Man Singh and machine guns! She got so terrified that when the poets, as was usual, said 'Vah! Vah!' after one particularly good line, she froze up for good. She plain stopped and sat down. The poets clapped. The audience remained silent.

The atmosphere was primed for poetry. The deep emotions of the love songs had got everyone in the mood for poetry. A poet recited some prose poetry. The audience took it in without making a peep. The next poet thought that the crowd was a little too silent. He looked at the screen of Shivaji. Everyone's attention fell on the image of the mounted Shivaji alongside the bathing beauties. Then the poet recited a war poem about Shivaji's battles, described the sacrifices of Guru Gobind Singh's sons, made sure to explain any difficult words and, in doing so, drew the repeated praise of the other poets. The Chairman promised to award him a medal. The poets clapped. Underneath the tent, two or three people followed suit. Then their clapping died in midstream. Aside from them, the audience remained silent. This irritated the next poet. He recited a very funny poem in a dramatic fashion in the local dialect. The other poets laughed. And there were some shows of interest in the crowd. That is, some laid their long staves down on the ground, and some relit their bidis. Even those who didn't write in the local dialect then decided to recite poems in that dialect. But this strategy grew quickly old. The laughter of those seated under the tent drew to a close. This silence really infuriated the poets. They started to remember nostalgically those festivals where crowds had hooted poets off the stage and had challenged the points of the Chairman's speech.

Finally, Pallauji recited some songs, and Ramanjore boasted to the police officers, 'He teaches at our school. He does good work. The kid's clever.' The crowds took in Pallauji's poetry in silence as well. Upon the insistence of the poets, MC Janardandas recited his pedagogical poem about Lord Vishnu's devotee Rantideva. Then, in his closing remarks, he joyfully announced the great success of the festival and praised the arrangements made by those responsible, Dasadin Sharma and Pallauji. Pallauji thanked the poets, thanked the crowd and then, at one in the morning, the festival was over. Everyone started leaving the stage. Gas lamps flickered near the screen of Shivaji and the bathing beauties.

But the crowd was still huddled under their blankets in the dew. Some lit their chillum pipes, and some stretched their legs. One of the police officers underneath the tree started cursing at one of the snack vendors. In the distance, Ramanjore cinched his long bandana around his waist. He could be heard screaming, 'Serve them some tea! Some tea! Over here!' Two boys sang the famous refrain of a ghazal from the nautanki play of the bandit Hamid Daku. People were starting to laugh and talk freely. From one end of the crowd, someone called out to someone else on the other side of the crowd. Some launched into domestic jokes and gibes. Dasadin Sharma saw what was going on, and he went back on stage.

'The festival is over,' he said. 'You all can go now!'

As soon as they heard this, the crowd grew restless. Clubs and sticks were raised. Blankets and quilts were thrown over shoulders, and everyone stood up. For a while, everyone shouted at one another. Then, simultaneously, everyone hushed. A revolt was brewing. Pandit Dasadin Sharma stood stock-still, silent and scared. After a bit more screaming, everyone sat down. Then a couple of young men, carrying clubs, approached Dasadin Sharma. They encircled him. Worried, Dasadin Sharma stammered, 'What is it? What do you people want?'

A muscular man stood proudly facing him. He had something to say. Seeing the man's pitch-black skin, pockmarked face, moustache with tips raised like a scorpion's stinger and neck swaying like a lizard's, Dasadin Sharma lost his wits. With a thud, the man placed his well-oiled, weighty club onto the ground. Dasadin Sharma's eyes bulged. He cleared his throat and was about to call out for help when this man raised his left hand toward his forehead in greetings, then very courteously asked, 'All of this was great, but, could you please tell me, Panditji, when will the real fun and games begin? When will the ticket collector return?'

4

Lucknow

It was the decline of the nobility and the rise of the coarse . . . Degradation was in the air. Debauchery was inaugurated . . . Prostitutes were everywhere . . . The quality in the marketplaces fell . . . Nothing was made from quality materials anymore . . . Rulers and leaders were worthless . . .

In front, Western-style shops, a movie theater, restaurants and a bar. Neon signs advertising gin, whiskey and beer spoke effectively of a ban on drinking water. Whenever an Impala emerged from out of the throng of Fiats and Ambassadors, we stood there entranced, our mouths agape, like when European coeds appear on the campuses of Indian universities. Fashionable, slender young women—

---

* An excerpt from *Fasana-e-ibrat* by Mirza Rajab Ali Beg 'Suroor' about the reign of Wajid Ali Shah's father Hazrat Amjad Ali Shah.

whose main goal in life is to attract the attention of idle young men, who in turn attract the attention of the police— walked down the street ostentatiously swaying from side to side. In front of the dazzling stores, street-smart young men with luxurious locks wearing loose bush shirts stuffed into tight bellbottoms sat like gigolos.

Hazratganj had become somewhat modernized. But this modernization was just like the type that you read about in stories where young Christian women are the only possible heroines.

I was standing in front of a new restaurant. With me were two journalists, a Hindi teacher and an emerging writer whose conviction didn't match his skill.

The Hindi teacher said, 'Hazratganj is becoming quite fashionable.'

In keeping with my innate desire to contradict, I said, 'To me, it looks rather countrified.' Then I told him why: 'This is the state capital. Shack and hut dwellers have come from far and wide to settle here. The Vidhan Bhavan is here. The cultures of all the villages and small towns from Kotdwara to Siswa Bazar are right here for you to see. Just go to a coffee shop. Step one foot inside and you'll think you're in a small-town barbershop. Everyone will be all up in your business. Everyone has a farmer's wily ways. No one will let you just be.'

This didn't sit right with the Hindi teacher. But since there was some deep truth hidden within my words, he accepted my statement as though it was one of Kabir's most hermetic poems and bit his tongue. Then he spoke about the modern art show taking place in the restaurant right behind me.

Inside, some wannabe artist was shamelessly using the restaurant for his gallery. Seated around a table, some intellectuals were desultorily talking about some problems. Without hearing what they were saying, I knew that neither their problems nor their thoughts were their own. The delusions inside the restaurant (the paintings and the intellectuals) were matched (as I've described) by the things outside the restaurant that belonged to the modern world of delusion.

But from where I was standing, modernity's shine was corroding because, in one direction, there was a cheap vegetarian thali restaurant for the lower and middle classes, and, in the other direction, a Hanuman temple where a handful of people had lost track of themselves and of Hanumanji and were singing Radha–Krishna devotionals. Without feeling the least shame, we offered prasad, got tilaks applied on to our foreheads, and moved on—just like the procedure for voting. We were silent exemplars of India's policy of neutrality.

Ahead of the temple, a new car was parked. Two men were seated inside. By the looks of it, they ate well, but drank even better. The vibe of insider trading, smuggling, income tax evasion, the corruption of youth and the wining and dining of government officials hung around their faces like halos in saint portraits. Then, suddenly, two glasses appeared in their hands, as though by magic. I watched them pour liquid from a bottle into the glasses and drink with great satisfaction.

'The Romantic era was the Dark Ages for Hindi poetry,' I said to the Hindi teacher, starting up some literary conversation.

This got under his skin. He wanted to say something on the behalf of Prasad, 'In contemporary world literature, compared to Prasad . . .'

'What do you know about contemporary world literature?' I needled him.

This upset him even more. 'What do you know about it?'

'I'm a Hindi writer,' I explained to him. 'So, you should expect that I read *Encounter* and *Times Literary Supplement*, which you do not.'

'Well, I read Prasad's literature, which you do not.'

I drew in my breath, then said, 'I'm a writer, and you're a teacher. We're not going to agree.'

So that he wouldn't have time to answer, I suddenly turned to my journalist friends to ask about the by-election. This brought me back to Lucknow.

The men in the car drank a second glass. From the vegetarian thali restaurant, a group of men with cracked heels and handlebar moustaches came out. From the Hanuman temple, loud cries rose up of 'Victory! Victory!' A Western car with plates from a different Indian state stopped and started, then broke through the traffic. It was being driven by a sketchy woman. The plate number and the state name were written in Hindi. Then, thankfully, our boredom was broken. Several Anglo-Indian young women came onto the sidewalk to stare at the Hanuman idol. Hanumanji returned their stare.

A rickshaw pulled up in front of us. We glimpsed the 16th century; I mean, a woman wearing a full burka. One of my journalist friends went up to the rickshaw. He wrinkled his nose several times, as though he smelled something bad. Then he came back and said to the other journalist, 'You go.'

'No,' the second journalist said. He gestured to me and said, 'He's going.'

'He's not going anywhere!' I said about myself.

'Then you go,' the second journalist said.

The first journalist got in the rickshaw and left.

It was 8 p.m.—evening in Britain, but night in India.

We started 'ganjing'. Like pregnant women, we strolled leisurely down the sidewalk, leaning on one another's shoulders. We slowed to a stop in front of the Gandhi Ashram, which sold actual honey made from real honeybees. One of my friends stopped to smoke a cigarette. A man in a dirty shirt and a pair of pants came up to us and asked for a cigarette. We started chatting politely. I asked him, 'What do you have up your sleeve today?'

He named a handful of demi-gods who could net a person one and a half thousand rupees or more. To prove his point, he took some star charts out of his pocket. Then, as required, he asked for my birth information. I said, 'I regret to inform you that I'm no longer in the income bracket that can support astrologers. If it comes to it, I ask a palm reader on the sidewalk, or a card reader.'

'So what? Take a chart.'

This time I spoke with great humility, 'It's not exactly that I can't support an astrologer, it's that right now I can't even support a wandering holy man.'

'So what?'

One of my journalist friends spoke up, 'And I regret that I can't buy you a beer. I'm completely out of money.'

The astrologer laughed, then said, 'No problem.' He began to fold up the star charts. I watched the fortunes of Uttar Pradesh's guiding lights slip into the pocket of his dirty pants.

After sharing a smoke, we returned to our leisurely stroll. Jokes were made about the astrologer. But I couldn't make any jokes about the attack of astrologers and wandering holy men on the capital. It reminded me of Rasputin's Russia. But I left things at that and started talking about something else.

From a nearby building, a gramophone was playing loudly. The message was to kill the Chinese and turn them away at the border. I remembered we were living during wartime. It was startling. Then we walked toward a paan stall. In the manner of someone stuck in a public-sector job, I said, 'If instead of my job, I could own a paan stall . . .'

'. . . then you'd still be selling paan,' one friend chimed in.

Then someone brought up the news that Ali Akbar Khan was going to have a concert in two days.

'In Lucknow?' I asked in surprise.

A little while later, a friend said that the night was still young. In fact, this is an artificial way of talking, but since we too were becoming artificial, talking like this felt quite natural.

We stopped walking and got into a car.

Then, in front of a park, we came to an open-air restaurant. There were chairs arranged on the sidewalk, and people were eating ice cream. We didn't get out, but we asked for cold soda and glasses to be brought over. We lounged alongside the park and breathed in the air circulating through the Gandhi statue, the new cars, the Chinese attacks and the liquor ads. We talked about Bhagvaticharan Verma, Amritlal Nagar and Yashpal. The government's niggling problems were discussed. The conversation turned intellectual.

By this time, there were only the three of us. We all had too much time on our hands—time was our biggest enemy. About a half hour later, we drove into a rich neighborhood where, several days before, a man had been killed in broad daylight. Someone had wanted to call the police, but the telephone-shop owner had forbidden him out of fear of the repercussions. Killing someone in broad daylight in the market isn't so much a sign of bad behavior as daring. What do you need to kill someone (or to become a politician) other than a little audacity? Talking the talk will help you walk the walk.

We passed through the shopping area known for daily goods—grain stores, general stores, vegetable stalls and street peddlers—and chanced upon a restaurant known in that neighborhood to be classy but, which to us, all snobs, looked third rate. Inside, we entered a big room: the dark paint on the walls was faded, and the flooring was fake marble. It felt like a cheap bar, through and through. We ordered coffee. A scantily clad waiter looked at us with surprise, then, having taken a minute to process our order, said, 'Okay, I'll see, I'll look into it.'

Then, a man holding a glass came up to our table to stare at me. 'Who are you?' he asked.

The man was from Old Lucknow. He was dripping with the aura of Ayurvedic medicine, second-hand nostalgia and worn-out ghazals.

'I'm a writer,' I said, full of dignity.

He stared at me. 'Do you write poetry?'

'No, but if I wanted to, I could.'

He stared at me a little longer. Then he said, 'You don't look the part.'

'That's because I shave and bathe every day.'

From the reaction on his face, it looked like I had fallen in his esteem. Then he pointed to a man in the corner and said, 'Do you know him? He's a modern master.'

He was right. In the nearby corner, one of the most famous tabla masters of our day was sitting, drinking alcohol. There were a couple other men seated there who, by the looks of it, were also musicians. As the tabla master drank, he cursed the times in which he lived, where tambourine players were considered percussionists on par with tabla players, and where All India Radio clamored after them!

The men seated around him nodded their heads in sad agreement.

He was sad. He mentioned Insha and Ghalib, either to name artists with universal recognition or for some other reason. I thought that I should say something, but then the old master, suddenly and without any prompting, put his hand to his ear and unleashed a ghazal. Several people goaded him into repeating it. His old voice was clear, clean and true. But when his voice rose in register, it never came back down. The room overflowed with energy and passion, and yet the meaning of the song was, in the end, that we were all doomed. It rubbed me the wrong way. And then

I remembered that I would need to get home soon. We pretended that we were in a hurry, and the waiter came back to tell us that we couldn't get coffee there.

We left. The streets were desolate. We left behind the richer neighborhoods. Far ahead were Aminabad, Maulviganj, Ashrafabad, Chauk and Nakhas Market—all closed for the night. A couple of boys, some women in burkas, some half-dead horses, some wobbly horse-drawn carts, some tobacco sellers and some halwa confectioneries were all you could find in that part of Lucknow, with some cauliflower and radish leaves rotting on the ground.

Old Lucknow was under siege. Yet the future wasn't controlled by a new generation. It was controlled entirely by old, clever hands, even if we weren't sure just whose hands they were. The young women with their form-fitting shalwars and messy hair who were walking so happily arm in arm along with the young men with their tight pants and baggy shirts looked ahead at the future with dreams of conquering all. But they were being controlled by those men sitting in Ambassador cars, sipping gin outside of the Hanuman temple, eating cheap vegetarian meals in keeping with the principles of non-violence.

I got out of the car near Hazratganj's Mayfair Cinema. I wanted to walk, and I was feeling emotional. I was thinking that if it were possible to know people's reaction to my death after having committed suicide, then suicide was definitely something to consider.

Walking alone, I came upon a beer ad that I couldn't turn away form. Past eleven at night, there was a young woman leaning on one of the billboard's poles. She was looking right, then left. From a distance, she looked like a young woman from the time of the old havelis, when young men wandered the night and there were families of old money.

I remembered a story published in the magazine *Maya* in which a prostitute used a sick brother as an excuse for her profession. She would tell clients that she had a brother who was sick and in the hospital.

I was walking by when she spoke to me. Her voice brought me back to reality. She asked what time it was. 'Eleven twenty-five,' I said. Then, without knowing why, I asked her if she had a sick brother.

'How did you know?' she asked, startled. Her voice was full of universal solidarity.

To answer her, I shrugged my shoulders, like Westerners do. I walked on. Our shadows crossed beneath the streetlights, and, like a shadow myself, I walked slowly home.

It was the end of one day in the life of a Lucknow intellectual.

5

Too Little, Too Late

Beating a dead horse has always been one of my hobbies. This time, it's a donkey. But still I'm hard at work beating it!

The issue at hand is Sahmat. In Ayodhya, Sahmat presented an exhibition on Ram's story. In it, there was a panel that presented the Buddhist Jataka tale, the 'Dashrath Jatak'. It contradicted Vaishnavite beliefs about Ram. Some cultural extremists avenged Sahmat's reasoning with the reckoning of the street, and they destroyed the 'Dashrath' panel. The dead horse was then carried to the newspapers where a hue and cry was raised. Then it was taken to parliament where it was beaten some more. Then the dead horse took to beating itself. Following close on the heels of the first blow, Sahmat gathered some well-known intellectuals and held a press conference.

At that point, the Ayodhya Police joined the fray. A police inspector at Ayodhya's main police station filed a preliminary charge sheet against Sahmat. The crime?

Wounding religious feelings and spreading social discord and insecurity.

This took place during the first week of August 1993. (In ten years, the beating of the dead horse will still be taking place.) The case was in the hands of the Central Bureau of Investigation, the CBI. Things were spinning out of control, and the CBI was being drawn into the mess.

So, in 1993, a CBI agent approached Sahmat's leader. A harsh interrogation followed.

'What wrong did we commit?' Sahmat's leader asked. 'We didn't write the "Dashrath Jatak", and the government hasn't banned the book. In any event, go find the person who wrote the book, and ask them your questions. And please charge them!'

'Who wrote it?'

'I don't know.'

'Who would know?'

'I don't know. Maybe Dr Weber would know. Or Dr Jacobi or Dinesh Chandra Sen.'

For several years, the CBI searched for these doctors. They perused every last Indian Medical Council registry but found nothing. Three years later, someone told them that these men weren't medical doctors but historians. This person also informed the CBI that these people were now residing in heaven. The CBI agents decided to seize copies of the 'Dashrath Jatak'.

They learned that the stories about Dashrath were in Pali. The CBI agents asked some geographers where Pali was. They found a region called Palia, but it had only two towns, Palia Kalan and Palia Khurd. There was no Pali. Then they learned that Pali was a language. When they accosted some Pali experts, they learned that the story 'Dashrath Jatak' was translated into Pali from Sinhalese, and the Sinhalese book may or may not still exist in Sri Lanka.

So, a joint director joined the CBI team, and soon they were in Sri Lanka. They looked far and wide for the book. They searched Buddhist monasteries, universities, libraries, bars, restaurants, cabaret halls, gambling dens . . . and where else? Who knows. But it was to no avail.

The CBI was given one piece of advice: *Don't think of this story of Ram as a report you can dictate in three hours. There are hundreds if not thousands of people behind it. And not just that, it's a part of a huge international conspiracy. Along with India, there's Tibet, Thailand, Cambodia, Malaysia, Java and Sumatra. Who knows how many countries are working together!*

The CBI thought the investigation should be turned over to the Research and Analysis Wing. But after searching the Buddhist monasteries, libraries, restaurants, etc., etc., etc. of Southeast Asia, they found a good fellow in Bangkok going by the name of Hanuman. He confirmed, 'Yes, that one, the one you're thinking about.'

He was asked about this and that, but Hanuman was more interested in bananas. He told the CBI team: 'You're barking up the wrong tree. You don't even know the rudiments of detective work. You haven't learned anything yet, so take my life as an example. Then you'll see how fake news—disinformation—is spread.'

He continued: 'Look at me. I was Lord Ram's lead agent—more important than even your director. You all know that I've been devoted to Ram since my youth. But stories of my love affairs have spread far and wide! If you don't believe me, then read the Seriram and Ramakien legends. Even in India, there are Jain tales in which I have thousands of wives!'

The joint director's face grew flushed with anger, 'What outrageous insolence!'

'No, it's not insolence. It's disinformation. They don't want you to see me as I really am. I mean, they're trying to turn the tried-and-true religious stories about me, the well-known ones, into a confusing maze you'll never emerge from. That's what "Dashrath Jatak" is doing too.'

The CBI withdrew from the investigation. The Research and Analysis Wing took over. Only now the government has grown tired of giving yearly grants to Sahmat, and so it has formally established a new department—the Shri Ram Harmonious Devotionals Directorate.

6

Angad's Foot

Although I dislike the ritual of going to the train station to see people off, in this instance, I had to go and bid farewell to a friend. This was due to several reasons. For one, he was a friend, and it's useless to argue about principles with friends. Second, he was going to travel first-class, and the thought of waving a handkerchief in front of the first-class cabin was very appealing to me.

So, I arrived at the station. I was one of many, many friends there to see my friend off. All of the workers in his division were there as well. The platform was bursting with life. Everywhere you looked, there was something happening. Since he always got to work on time, he got to the station right on time, as well. All of his subordinates had garlands in their hands, and they hung them around his neck. He shook everyone's hands. He exchanged two or three words with everyone. And then he stood right next to the first-class compartment so that there was no danger of the train leaving without him.

The train was scheduled to leave. Everyone was looking ahead at the signal light. But it was red.

Since there was nothing more to do, my friend chose one man from out of the crowd to talk to. He was the man who insincerely invited everyone to his house, and whose invitations were put off with an insincere laugh by each and every person he invited. My friend had done so as well. My friend said, 'Next time I'll come stay at your house.'

The man started to laugh, 'My house is your house. Just tell me when you're coming. I'll send a car to the station.'

'There's no need for a car!'

'Really, sir, the car's yours. There's no need to stand on ceremony!'

'I'm not standing on ceremony—we're like family.'

'Okay, sir, if you're part of the family, then you really must come share a dinner at our humble abode.'

'What are you talking about? I only ever eat at your house!'

Then they started laughing.

I didn't pay the slightest attention to this conversation because my friend always stayed at my house, and nothing was going to change that.

My friend always got to work on time, but he would always leave late.

Then the train whistle blew, startling everyone. Everyone stared in the direction of the signal. Yet the train didn't budge.

So, with the delay, people started up on the standard subjects: please write to everyone when you get home; the guavas are so good where you live, please bring some back when you return. The elderly servant said that he had put the snacks behind the bed sheets. Then the elderly head clerk said that he had spread sheets over the train seat. Then the accountant said that it would be better to change the position of the head of the bed so that the coal smoke wouldn't be a problem. Then the head clerk said no, there would be no coal smoke as things were, and you would get to enjoy the scenery. Then the cashier came up to my friend and gave him ten rupees in change. Then, full of friendliness, my friend patted him on the shoulder and thanked him.

But the one thing that was supposed to happen didn't happen.

People had known for a month that my friend was going to leave so whatever of meaning they had had to say, they had already said in private, and now what they said in front of everyone was simply what everyone says to others in public.

The luggage was on board. The ticket was bought. The garlands had been placed around his neck. He had either shaken hands with eveyrone or hugged them—or both— and yet the train was still there. It was as though the hero had raised his dagger above the villain while glaring at him, and yet the curtain didn't descend. What was the audience to think? It was like that. The play refused to end.

Since I had nothing more to say to my friend, I left his side to go find someone with whom my friend could talk comfortably. When I found a candidate, I pushed him over to my friend. With his perpetual smile, the man said, 'Our club will feel deserted after you leave.' My friend laughed off this compliment. Then the man said, 'In Mr Brown's time, tennis was popular, but then it lost its popularity. In your time here, it started to become popular again, but now look what has happened!' My friend said, 'What's there to worry about? You take the reins.' The man got very upset. He flew into a rage, 'Sir, what can I possibly do? I don't want these boys, not even for club secretary! Tennis won't get off the ground with a foolish secretary! I'm ready to get rid of them all!' He stood there defiantly. My friend laughed the matter off. After that, the conversation petered out into nothingness.

But still the train hadn't left.

My friend looked helplessly at the signal for several minutes. Some people started wandering the platform smoking cigarettes and chewing paan. Some were so obsessed by international news so they wandered over to the bookstall to flip through newspapers. Some were suddenly beset by a love for art, crafts and rural industries. They went into a nearby store to look at the local handicrafts. Then a local station-worker went up to my friend. The man's appearance made my friend suddenly start believing in socialism. He laughed and then complimented the man. The man cried and then told my friend all about his family's hardships. My friend listened to him with great compassion. Then a ticket-checker emerged from the crowd and then disappeared. My friend watched him go. In the amount of time it took to wet his lips to call out, the ticket-checker had already disappeared, and a tall guard stepped forward blowing a whistle. The head clerk addressed him, 'Listen, sir . . .'

The guard ignored him and, blowing his whistle, disappeared.

But still the train hadn't left.

Some people took pity on my friend and surrounded him. After sorting themselves out, several little groups formed, and if there's 'art for art's sake', they started up on 'conversation for conversation's sake'.

One man's glance fell on my friend's garland. He praised it. He said, 'How beautiful marigold garlands are! A real flower garland can only be made with marigolds.'

Once an old motor kicks to life, there's no stopping it!

A second man said, 'In India, we haven't stopped using water buffalos to pull carts, and marigold garlands are the same. Water buffalo carts are our cars, peda are our sweets and marigolds are our flowers—that, sir, is Indian culture!'

Then, from the edge of the crowd, a third man bellowed, 'The British have left, but they forgot to take their bastard children with them!'

A retort followed: 'Yes, Indians like you still exist, but your mind isn't right.'

Then, in order to avoid the next round of insults, the first man turned to address my friend, 'Sir, tell me, out of the varieties of roses . . .'

Then the guard blew his whistle, and, startled, everyone looked in the engine's direction. The engine was wheezing. For a couple of seconds, the sound continued, then the train returned to its previous state, exactly its previous state. It was in the same manner as my friend, who, before leaving the office, would get up, see a new piece of paper on his desk, then sit back down.

The flower lover started up again, 'Sir, as I was saying, the British have come up with so many varieties of roses. Sunburst, Pearl, Lady Hillingdon, Black Prince—it's amazing! It's just wonderful! And here? Here, there's just our old little rose, but what a sweet scent it has!'

Before anything more could be said, the guard blew his whistle. No one spoke.

But still the train didn't budge.

So, the second man pushed through the crowd. He reached my friend and the other man. He spoke disdainfully, 'Sir, could we please return to what you were saying about my mind. My mind is Indian, but what about yours?'

Then my friend laughed loudly and said, 'Hatim Bhai and Saxena Sahib are always going at it like this! I'll remember this—I'll remember this fight!'

So the matter was resolved, and they were forced to abandon their fight. The signal switched. The engine whistled.

But still, like Angad's foot, the train was stuck in place.

At the back of the crowd, a philosophy professor was slowly explaining to a friend, 'Sir, life is three-quarters oppression, which is the stranglehold of coercion. The remaining quarter is okay. You see, all I need is a takht, but for others I have to put a sofa in the living room. A dhoti is all I need for clothes, but, then, to go out, I have to wear a suit. This is coercion. This is life. I drink coffee, even though I prefer the taste of milk. I want to read spy novels, but I read Kant and Hegel instead. I suffer from arthritis, but I come stand at the station for hours waiting to say goodbye to friends.'

He and his interlocutor laughed as though they were sharing a secret, and then they scooted closer to me and began laughing so loudly that I wouldn't be able to mistake the signs of their restlessness.

But still the train hadn't budged.

Now the crowd was growing agitated. My friend had the same pathetic smile plastered on his face that you can probably see when people lie to their sons, or steal money from their wife's purse to go watch a movie or when on the campaign trail they promise voters such-n-such a future. It was like he wanted to smile, but he also didn't want to look anyone in the eye.

The guard blew his whistle. He waved the flag. The engine sounded its horn. The train started moving. People reached enthusiastically for my friend's hand. My friend boarded the train, then reached out to shake hands. Some people started waving handkerchiefs. I had been so looking forward to this scene! I wanted to get out my handkerchief, but, like always, I had forgotten it at home. So I waved goodbye with my hand.

As soon as the guard blew his whistle, the one man who had been wasting time by weighing himself on a scale and watching as others weighed themselves, raced forward and pushed his way all the way up to my friend. As the train left the station, he reached out to shake my friend's hand. Having confirmed that the train was truly leaving the station, he said in a voice full of regret, 'Too bad you can't stay for longer!'

7

Interview with a Defeated Politician

When I arrived at his bungalow, I mistook him for a piece of furniture on the verandah. He was standing there like Napoleon after his defeat at Waterloo. A dried-out lawn lay in front of the bungalow. Several dust-covered jeeps were parked there. Old car parts and tires were strewn about.

Inside an open shed, four sets of loudspeakers and some worn-out carpets lay in a heap. To the side, bamboo poles and sticks were scattered on the ground. I could see a handful of gunnysacks inside the shed, but I couldn't tell if they were full of knives or liquor bottles.

On the verandah, a breeze riffled a stack of posters. Election ballots blew this way and that.

I told him that I was a reporter. He said that he'd already lost the election and vacated his seat. 'I can't give you anything now . . .' he said.

I said that he could give me an interview.

To encourage him, I said that his situation was like that of Napoleon: he had lost, but he wasn't dead. 'In this situation,' I said, 'even if you aren't able to do anything else, you can still give an interview. Just look at your fellow elder statesmen. For years now, what have they done for the country other than give interviews?'

He agreed. 'Give me a couple minutes. Let me get my gadgets.'

He was eighty-two years old. Actually, up till then, I had been shouting into his ear. He rang a bell for his servant. He put in his false teeth, put on a pair of glasses and inserted a large hearing aid into one ear. As soon as he did this, he looked exactly like how he was depicted in caricatures. He sat slouched in a comfortable armchair in a position somewhere between lying and sitting, between living and dead.

'I was very sad to hear about your defeat,' I said.

'A lot of people have said this to me, even ones who voted against me.'

'That's no surprise,' I began to explain. 'Actually, the masses are passing through an upsetting time. Even if you had won, they would have been upset. So, you lost, and still they were upset.' Then I asked a question, 'What are your plans now?'

'To give an interview, as you already know.'

'I understand. But several days ago, the newspapers said that you had renounced politics.'

'That's wrong. What I said was that religious renunciates should join politics too.'

His answers were full of wit. It seemed as though his mind wasn't a part of his body—as though, like his teeth, it had been attached prosthetically.

'So, you'll continue to be active in politics?'

'If I'd won, you wouldn't be asking. Other that politics, what's there for me to do?'

'You've been active in politics for more than a half century. It doesn't get boring?'

'We call it service to the country,' he said in a serious tone, then his mouth went slack.

'You don't think it best to let a new generation into politics?'

With great effort, he raised his head. For a moment, he stared at the ceiling. 'Where's the new generation? I don't see them anywhere.'

I was taken aback. I asked again, 'So, in your opinion, there's no young people in the entire country?'

This seemed to irk him a little. He answered sharply, 'There must be! There must be somewhere! But I don't know them.'

'And you think that in the masses there's not a single person who . . .'

He interrupted me, 'The masses? The masses must be out there somewhere! But I don't know them.'

In order to let him cool down, I said nothing. And, after a while, he regained his compsure. Then I asked, 'What do you think the reason for your defeat was? To what extent do you think it can be considered a defeat of your policies?'

He thought for a moment. Then he said, 'Look, this can't be a defeat of my policies because I don't have any.' Quickly, he added, 'But it wasn't out of love.'

He tried to explain the situation, 'No one likes to say they were defeated, it's better to say it wasn't me, it was my policies that were the problem. Then the stain of defeat is one step removed.'

'So what was the reason? Caste politics?'

'I don't have any problem with caste politics. I've been elected several times on the back of caste politics.' He nodded his head, 'The real reason for my defeat is Saturn and Rahu. Policies, principles, the people's mood—that's always what people say. But, really, it was the planets that did me in. And I knew it beforehand. A full seven astrologers warned me that Saturn and Rahu were in transit in the twelfth house, and Mars could be clearly seen above them.'

He stopped for a moment. 'You don't believe in astrology? This is our sages' great blessing—the science of astrology!'

I didn't bother answering his question. Instead, I asked, 'Why then did you contest the election knowing what the astrologers had said?'

'There was no way around it!' he said. Then he added, 'It's because of the planets! Jupiter was ascendant, sitting in the fourth house, looking straight at the tenth house! How was I supposed to win in such inauspicious conditions?'

Now I finally understood. He intended to journey through the solar system, visiting each and every planet, just so long as it wasn't Earth. I closed my notebook, said thanks and got up. He was still saying something about astrology.

I interrupted him, finally speaking my piece, 'People are suffering. It would be good to give them a message of hope—of *asha*.'

Maybe he didn't hear me. He looked in my eyes and asked, full of distress, 'Asha? Do you know her? Where does she live now?'

I had heard enough. There was no need to push me out the door.

8

One Happy Day

I got up early and washed. I took out a shirt and a clean pair of pants from the laundry and, to my surprise, saw that there were no missing buttons. I glanced into the corner of the room where my shoes were. Our servant had an old habit of using the red brush to polish my shoes, but this time he had actually used the correct brush. Right then, I said to myself that it was going to be a happy day.

I got on the bus going to the college, and I gave the conductor a one-rupee note. I got back the correct change, and he didn't write an 'I owe you' worth one anna on the back of the ticket. When I sat down, it wasn't next to a woman, and so I was freed from my weakness for reading about the romantic entanglements of the stars of the film world. I spread out my legs and relaxed. A man seated next to me was reading a newspaper. I glanced his way, and he lifted the paper so I couldn't look at him. I looked at the day's headlines. No foreign power had given India any development technology, no speech had come down from the prime minister. For one day, the paper wouldn't bore me to death. I started reading.

At the railway crossing, the guard saw the bus coming and didn't put down the gate. The bus passed by without impediment, as though this was a daily occurrence. When the bus stopped near the college, I got off without having to push anyone, without bumping knees with anyone, without having to say 'thank you' and 'sorry'. Of course, there was a man selling chaat at the bus stand, but he didn't see me, and he didn't try to entice me with his 'hot hot chaat!'

I spent a happy day at the college. To the boys, I read an essay about my trip to Europe. In the next class, I expounded upon the glory of virtue. I didn't have to tell a love story, and I didn't have to explain the meaning of any witty satire. No female student told me a sentimental story or recited a poem over the course of an hour that would force me to revise her grade. No sycophantic students came to praise some mediocre work of mine. No lecturer called me 'Amma yaar' in front of the students. Students came out of the room of a rival lecturer shouting for a revolution. In the staff room, I heard some choice anecdotes about the principal, and they didn't come from me.

Before going home, a friend picked me up to go have tea at a fancy restaurant. He let me talk, and he listened for practically the whole time. In front of the restaurant, I reached into my pocket for money to pay the rickshaw driver. I found a ten-rupee note, but my friend had already found the correct change in his pocket. Inside, there was no hassle. The waiter wasn't the old, stuffed, overbearing sort. Instead, he was a timid neophyte. At the nearby tables, there were no wisecracking youth, no fashionable young ladies and no uproarious guffaws. No one was staring at me, and no one was whispering about me. The restaurant wasn't that busy, but it wasn't empty either, and so the manager behind the counter didn't have the opportunity to stare intently at us. Before we left, two serious-looking men sat down at a nearby table, and when I happened to use the word 'existentialism' in conversation, they looked over at me. After leaving the restaurant, my eyes fastened upon an insurance agent who I knew who was walking down the street, but he didn't see me. Then I ran into three men I knew. They said hello and went on their way. My friend didn't run into anyone he knew.

When I got home, I asked my wife if she wanted to go to the cinema, but she said that she was sorry she had a get-together with friends already arranged. So I was able to go ahead with my plan to go to the movies with my friend. This time we were actually able to get tickets from the cinema's ticket counter at the correct price. We got seats right under a ceiling fan. Before the movie, there were no commercials for soap, oil or Vanaspati ghee. There was no one nearby blowing cigarette smoke into my face. No one behind me put his feet up on the back of my seat. No one elbowed me in the dark. No one started sobbing because of the hero's plight. It was a Hindi film, but it finished before the end of its eighteenth reel. Outside after the film, rickshaw drivers didn't accost me. Without being forced into a rickshaw, I was able to walk home. While I walked home on the quiet night road, no bicyclist rammed into me, no motorist cursed at me and no policeman gave me a fine.

At home, having sat down to eat, I didn't have to listen to my wife talk about our financial problems. Our servant didn't get mad. I spoke on and on about literature, I mean, I kept lambasting writers I knew. My wife listened with great interest and didn't intuit my pettiness.

The entire house was peaceful. There was no light bulb that had unexpectedly burnt out, no pipe that had burst without reason; there was no guest shouting at the front door, no sound of a plate dropped on the kitchen floor; there was no poetry festival being broadcast over the radio, no religious songs blaring from a loudspeaker in the neighborhood. And the best thing about all of this was that the next day would be Sunday, and all of my over-enthusiastic friends were going on a picnic together somewhere far from the city.

9

Meeting a Victorious Politician

For those who have read my 'An Interview with a Defeated Politician', you will recall how the defeated politician was over eighty years old and did the business of politics with the help of various sense aids, I mean, glasses, dentures, hearing aids and so on. But my optimism was reborn when I met the victorious politician and witnessed his abrasive, unpolished and energetic personality. Meeting the defeated politician, I thought the country would soon go to hell. Meeting the victorious politician, I became convinced that our country is on the road to heaven.

Although this politician was neither especially young nor a Turk, his followers called him a young Turk. He was around fifty-five years old, but in the hundreds of youth clubs and student organizations that he visited, he was right at home. He spoke in a clear, loud voice, and he was voluble. Because he talked so much, people thought that he was full of ideas, and, as soon as he opened his mouth, whatever came out of his mouth was mistaken for one. When he had the chance to get out of his car and walk, he walked very fast. He thought that people would see his brisk pace and think of Mahatma Gandhi's morning walks, even if his fast pace made some people think of pickpockets.

We hoped that after getting elected, this politician would become a minister, and that our country would take to heart the example of his brisk walks and start to pick up the pace too. But he wasn't made a minister, or, if you will, he didn't become a minister. Whatever the case may be, since a close friend of his was already a minister, he became *like* a minister. And since his close friend was a very simple man who hesitated to step out of the shadows of administrators and astrologers in order to meet the actual people, slowly, this man was downgraded to being only like a minister, and our speedy politician rose from being like a minister to become *more or less* the minister.

In any event, being like a minister is prestigious enough, and, at his house—which suddenly everyone called a 'bungalow'—there were hundreds of people milling around from dawn till dusk. It was known that you didn't need either any bribe or any special letter of introduction in order to speak to him. All you needed were strong shoulders and healthy lungs to push through the crowds. I had also heard about how he never got wrapped up in right or wrong, moral or immoral. Like a true believer, he put his head down and produced results. I mean, he got others to do for others. Being like a minister, he was the bellows that starts the fire.

A crowd was forming at the gate to his house. Actually, people had climbed onto the gate, and some others were hanging from it. To one side, there was a big mango tree, with one branch just four or five feet above the ground. People were sitting on it. On the road leading to the house's portico, there were country folk with their little blankets and towels spread out on the ground. They were sitting there waiting. It looked like the indolent crowd outside a cricket stadium when a test match is being played inside. As I made my way to the portico, I noticed that there were people sitting on every tree in the vicinity, and standing on or swinging from its branches. I had to use my shoulders and lungs several times to press through the crowd, but on the way to the portico a man posing as an insider said to me, 'Go ahead, Babu Sahib is seated on the portico. The crowd isn't too bad today, you'll get to see him soon.'

He was right. There was no car under the portico, only twenty or so chairs arranged haphazardly. On average, there were two people seated in each chair. In between these chairs, there was our politician, the hope of the young, the Young Turk, the *kind-of* minster. He had his legs spread out in front of him, the upper half of his body was covered in a dirty bath towel and there was soap all over his face. He was being shaved.

The phone next to him rang over and over, and he had to interrupt what he was saying to pick it up. In the meantime, the barber stood to the side and resharpened his razor. As soon as he hung up, he started talking to a new petitioner while he urged the barber to hurry up. When the chance came, the barber would run the blade once or twice over the politician's cheek or chin, then step back and wait for him to stop talking.

I stood to the side. The politician's eyes never stopped scanning the scene. When he saw me, he said, 'Don't stand over there. Sit down.' Then the refrain 'sit down, sit down' descended upon me from all corners. 'Sit down with someone,' he said. 'What can I say? No matter how many chairs we put out, there still aren't enough.' He looked up helplessly at the barber who sprang to action to shave the stubble off his right cheek. When the politician opened his mouth to say something, the barber raised the blade straight up into the sky and stepped away. Then the politician said, 'I was speaking to you! Hurry up with your shaving. Hurry up and finish.' He showed the barber the other side of his neck, then spoke to someone casually, 'What do you need?' (He spoke casually to everyone.) The man said, 'Please get Bhurelal transferred.' The politician spoke, 'Okay, I will, but remember Bhurelal is a first-class scoundrel. What's he to you?' 'Sir, he's my son.' The politician spoke plainly, 'So set him straight. If not, some day you'll find him hanging from a tree. Now go put him straight. There's not much time to talk today. You'll get your wish. Secretary, please make of a note of this.'

A man who looked like a secretary wrote something down in a big book. The man with whom I was sharing a corner of a chair spoke up, 'He got his wish.' I asked, 'How do you know?' 'Didn't you see him write it down in the register?' Then the politician was speaking to someone else, 'You're always coming with these little things. "Find so-and-so a job as a maid", "Find so-and-so a job as a clerk." I'm the only person you can ask?' The politician's second cheek was still covered with foam. Only one cheek was clean shaven. Putting the two cheeks together, it was a clown's face. I thought it was the perfect representation of the country's politicians.

The petitioner stood up. He spoke, 'Since you can turn someone into a clerk just like that, please get Baijnath a good job. Please get him a job as a collector, or make him an ambassador somewhere.' The politician laughed, 'Secretary, please make a note of it: find Baijnath a job as an ambassador.' Then he spoke to the crowd, 'With your blessings and support, some day I'll make you all ambassadors!'

No one said 'nay' to that.

'What do you want?' the politician asked. 'Speak quickly, I'm about to leave.'

I realized he had been talking to me. I stepped forward.

'Just say it from there,' he said, turning to speak to someone else. Then he looked back at me. 'Speak up, now's your chance,' he said.

I thrust forward a piece of paper, 'The Minister told me that . . .'

'You want a Fiat, right? No worries, I'll get you one,' he interrupted me.

'No, it's not that.'

'A scooter? You'll get it, but it'll take six months. Give your name to the secretary. Case closed.' Then he started speaking to someone else.

I stepped forward and spoke, 'In my village, there's been no doctor for the past two years. Someone needs to be placed there.'

'Placed there? You want to go?' he asked me.

'Please send any old doctor whatsoever.'

'Speak clearly now. Should I appoint you?'

'I'm not a doctor.'

'So then your boy? Your nephew? Just tell me who, and I'll make it happen.'

'There are no doctors in the family. We just need a real doctor there.'

The politician screamed, 'Secretary, listen to him and write down whatever he wants. I can't figure out what he's saying.' For a second, his anger overwhelmed him. He fell silent, and, in that moment, the barber set to finishing his job.

Suddenly, a woman's voice thundered from somewhere inside the house. People flooded out of the doors for what must have been the living room, bedroom and bathroom. They came out to sit under the portico or on the lawn. Just like a shepherdess tends to her flock, a woman followed them onto the verandah. She was rather pretty, but, due to all her yelling, her voice was unpleasant to listen to.

The politician smiled, then said, 'Things are so bad that people will wait in the bathroom to ambush me with what they have to say. And this poor woman has to spend her entire day flushing them out.' Then he rushed over to the verandah and patted his wife on the shoulder, saying, 'Don't worry. I'll be finished in two minutes.'

The bathroom seemed to be at one end of the verandah. He started walking in that direction in order to take care of the petitioners who were seated there and to wash up with his wife. He started unbuttoning his shirt as he walked.

A man who looked like a professor was standing under the portico. He said, 'Too bad he wasn't made a minister. They would have no way of saying no to his dynamism.'

10

More Like a Swami Than a Swami

The former city manager was famous for eating too much paan and taking too many bribes. And so, to punish him, he was given a new job as the state's finance minister. The new city manager was different: he didn't eat paan. And yet complaints didn't subside, the city was lost in a maze of poor planning, and it seemed a plot was underfoot to tarnish the image of the honorable prime minister.

So immediately after taking oath of office, the new urban development minister launched a surprise investigation into the city and the city administration. He took with him a government photographer and two reporters, even though they weren't government sponsored.

On site, he found that one engineer, two deputy administrators and three assistant administrators were absent. He announced their transfers on the spot. The engineer had already been given his transfer papers, but the high court had postponed the transfer, and so he still had his job. The enginner was chewing paan at the paan store outside the gates, and as soon as he heard that the minister had handed down new transfer orders, he flew off to the high court to file a defamation suit against the minister. There, he met the two deputy and three assistant administrators who were filing for delays on their reassignments.

Seeing the minister appear in his office, the city manager was flabbergasted by the unexpectedness of the inspection.

The minister bellowed, 'Come on now, where's your discipline? There's no one here! Your administration is shit! The whole city is rotting away beneath the filth and garbage. The city's a big trash heap.'

The city manager politely asked the minister to sit down. Then he said, 'You're completely right, sir. This is exactly what I faced when I came to this job. But we're trying to rejuvenate the city with all our might. We want to make it a model town of the twenty-first century . . .'

The invocation of the twenty-first century stopped the minister cold in his tracks.

The ensuing conversation went a little like this:

MINISTER: The whole city smells like shit. There are missing manhole covers everywhere. When it floods, the water brings the trash with it . . .

CITY MANAGER: Sir, the sewer problem is dire. It was built for a city of 300,000. But now the population is 1.3 million, and, by the turn of the twenty-first century, it will be 2.1 million. We've asked the World Bank for a loan of 503,700,000 rupees, which will bring in some innovative technology from Japan and Italy. Another thing is . . .

MINISTER: Trash is heaped on the streets. What's your staff doing about that?

CITY MANAGER: Sir, our old garbage trucks and staff work every day, ten hours a day. In three days, they can remove only 5,000 tons of trash, but the city generates 30,000 tons of waste each week. Analyzing the city's total trash production, we have made provisions in the next five-year plan, taking on the Washington Pattern . . .

MINISTER: Enough, enough. What about the water problem? The western neighborhoods haven't got a drop of water in three days, and you're at home in your bungalow, napping.

CITY MANAGER: This problem, too, sir, is a result of the bad planning of the last administration. Based upon the survey of the World Health Organization, the central government and the State Planning Commission, we have formed an initiative that the next seven years will lead to 1,200,000 additional gallons of capacity . . .

MINISTER: Not another initiative!

CITY MANAGER: And as far as the bungalow is concerned, sir, I don't have one. There is a 1,242,000-rupee provision for the building of a residence for the city manager. With a new residence, the city manager's abilities can be expected to increase by 35.7 per cent.

MINISTER: The roads are full of potholes! Transfer the chief engineer immediately.

CITY MANAGER: Sir, there is no chief engineer. The public service commission is going to advertise the job next month. To fix the roads, we've submitted an initiative, asking for 1,230,000 rupees to the state, in which . . .

MINISTER: Even if you get this money, there's so much corruption here . . .

CITY MANAGER: Sir, the problem of corruption relates to human resources, planning and moral climate. It's a universal problem. But we've put together a top-flight team to address it.

(The MINISTER gets up.)

MINISTER: Shut up! I'm talking about the current conditions of the city, and you're citing statistics for your upcoming plans like you're on television reporting the news!

CITY MANAGER: Sir, it's very important to report the news on television. The news tells people about the present conditions and about what India will look like in the future. In fact, I take my inspiration for building the city's future from the news. But, from now on, we'll also have your valuable leadership. Now everyone living in the city should be full of hope that our young prime minister will lead the city into the twenty-first century . . .

The reporters on duty were busy taking these notes when the door opened and snacks were brought in—coffee and cashews.

11

Pandit, Thakur, Lala, Babu, Munshi, Etc.

Take it from me that when Prime Minister Rajiv Gandhi once again refers to the late Prime Minister Jawaharlal Nehru as 'Panditji', it's not that he's launching himself into the ultra-modern twenty-first century, but rather it's nothing more than the beginning of an election year. In an election year, Brahmins need to be reminded that although Panditji studied in England, his family members were all dyed-in-the-wool Brahmins. But to claim that Rajiv Gandhi made Nehru a pandit would be going too far. By never referring to him in public as 'nana', he never stooped to idle flattery. That's all that can be said about what he did. For example, in parliament, he announced the 'Jawahar Employment Initiative', not the 'Nana Employment Initiative'.

On the other hand, the other day in the Lok Sabha, he did say 'Mom' and not 'Indiraji', reminding everyone that he is the only surviving son of his late mother. These are sad matters, but what I mean to say is that to get the most number of votes possible, it's best for him to refer to his grandfather as 'Panditji' and refer to the last prime minister Indira Gandhi as 'Mom'. In one fell swoop, he can make himself out to be a regular government employee and his family's little boy.

I've nothing more to say about the current prime minister. I mentioned him only in the context of the word 'Panditji', and here my essay is called 'Pandit, Thakur, Lala, Babu, Munshi, Etc.' Everyone knows that Jawharlal started to be called Panditji a long time ago, in the time of the British. The British in Cambridge didn't call him Panditji to make fun of him; rather it was due to British cultural influence and etiquette in India that he was called that.

The rule of etiquette was this: give a respectful title to important public figures which is connected to their caste: for Brahims, Pandit; for Rajputs, Thakur; for Kayasthas, Babu and sometimes Munshi; and for Baniyas, Lala. For Shudras and other backward castes, all of this wasn't necessary because there weren't enough of them in public life, and if the need ever arose, then 'Babu' worked well enough, like Babu Jagjivan Ram.

Politicians always used to have something in front of their name other than 'Shri' or 'Mister'. Pandit Madan Mohan Malviya, Chaudhuri Charan Singh, Thakur Hukum Singh, Babu Rajendra Prasad, Babu Jayaprakash Narayan, Lala Lajpat Rai. In this tradition, there is Jawaharlal Nehru too, whom everyone was happy to call a Brahmin and touch his feet, but who became 'Pandit' to the extent that his grandson can call him 'Panditji' without the slightest hesitation.

This rule of etiquette wasn't limited to politicians, lawyers, doctors and so on. (In their professional life, doctors escaped being called Pandit, Lala, Babu and so on. With 'Doctor' in front of their name, a respectful caste title became unnecessary.) This rule of etiquette applies only to the most important people in the fields of literature and education: Pandit Mahavir Prasad Dvivedi, Babu Shyamsundar Das, Thakur Gopal Sharan Singh, Lala Sitaram Bhup and, last (and most importantly), Munshi Premchand.

Today we know him as Munshi Premchand. It's another matter altogether that this rule of etiquette doesn't hold true for his children. We don't say Munshi Shripat Rai or Munshi Amrit Rai, and even though Rajiv Gandhi calls Jawaharlal Nehru 'Panditji', we don't call him Babu Rajiv Gandhi.

Beyond literary figures, artists and their ilk, this rule of etiquette applied to government service well, though here too there were exceptions. Without these exceptions, the list of government officials—the civil list—would have made for an interesting read. In 1949, when I entered into civil service, the list of slightly older applicants had just missed out on becoming IAS officers read like a register at a strange zoo: Pandit Ramkrishna Trivedi, Babu Mahavir Sharan Das, Thakur Jaykirat Singh, etc. But these lists were all before Independence. After Independence, this rule of etiquette, in which a caste name was placed before a personal name, was dropped, and so I just escaped being called Pandit Shrilal Shukla in government records.

Now for the exceptions. In government service, the first exception is for work in an all-India service branch.

If you're in the ICS or IPS, there's no need for Pandit, Babu, Lala and so on. If you're in the ICS, then it's assumed you've gotten over the barrier of Pandit, Lala and so on. So, if one man was B.P. Bagchi, ISO, his brother could have been Pandit Gauriprasad Bagchi, Deputy Collector.

Another exception was for plaintiffs and defendants. In a courtroom, there were no pandits and babus. For litigants, only your given name counted, and it was usually announced in court in a rude, brusque and incorrect way.

The logic behind the third exception is a little difficult to explain. This unspoken rule of etiquette is mainly a North Indian tradition, one of Uttar Pradesh (then United Provinces), Bihar, Madhya Pradesh, Punjab and other states. Maharashtra (then Bombay, or Greater Bombay) was not affected by this rule of etiquette, so, Bal Gangadhar Tilak never had to affix Pandit before his name. B.B. Kher, Murarji Desai, S.K. Patel—they all were unaffected by the honorific that marked nobility from the time of Lala Lajpat Rai to Pandit Jawaharlal Nehru.

The south remained entirely impervious to all of this. Chakravarti Rajagopalachari, Pattabhi Sitaramayya, K. Kamaraj and others—could they be given the titles of Pandit or Lala? All in all, this rule of etiquette was an excess of northern culture.

Why? Only historians or sociologists can say for sure. I can only guess. The real and dire consequences of the rebellion of 1857 were felt only in North India. The British imperialists still considered this area to be dangerous, and so they adopted some subtle strategies to prevent the development of solidarity among the people.

So, this beautiful etiquette of naming Pandit, Babu, Lala, Munshi and so on—wasn't it a part of these subtle strategies? Wasn't it a part of the effort by people in power to undercut the broad goal of a single, united society? By parceling out the names Pandit, Thakur, Babu, Lala and so on, wasn't it a concerted effort to divide society by petty caste politics?

It was in that social context that the current prime minister's great-grandfather became Pandit Motilal Nehru; and, in the twentieth century, when his grandfather came back from Cambridge, he too was awarded the title of pandit despite his obviously Westernized ways. I don't know if the title's a blessing or a curse, but by the easy manner with which the word is tossed around even today, it seems like the titles of Pandit, Thakur, Chaudhuri, Babu, Lala, Munshi and so on are just as respected as new technology, the principles of socialism and the dreams of a classless, casteless society.

You'll probably be filled with an idealistically holy anger while thinking about how yours truly is making these comments about caste based upon so little evidence. But please don't forget that this is an election year in which all political parties are emphasizing the need to become a casteless, classless society, and all around us there are preparations underway to lay siege to the pettiness of class and caste interests. So, as long as we have time, perhaps it's not the worst thing to think about what this business of Pandit, Lala, Thakur, Baba, Chaudhuri, Munshi is all about.

12

Doordarshan's Worldview

Have you ever seen a politician taking a bribe? I have. In a Doordarshan episode of 'This is Life'. I loved it, and so I'm waiting to see a chief minister take a bribe in the next episode, and then someone else after all—please forgive me for saying so!

But there will be no need to wonder what will happen next. In countless interesting shows, Doordarshan has already provided so many examples of bribery and other forms of cheating and deceit that it can now be counted as a terrifying social norm. Just as mosquitos have become immune to the continuous application of DDT, we have become numb to corruption—all due to Doordarshan's theatrics. In the future, we will accept corruption as a form of derring-do in the way that some young men see rape depicted over and over in films and start to think of it as an acceptable form of passionate lovemaking.

There is one more benefit in Doordarshan's policy to expose corruption. It bursts the opposition's bubble. Now who will listen when the opposition tells stories about corruption? When intellectuals tell the same stories? Will the masses listen? Doordarshan has already told them everything! Will the government listen? The government has known from the beginning, and the government is the one informing the masses!

So, what should opposition journalists and intellectuals do?

They should support Doordarshan's 'Rajani' series! In fact, according to the mission statement of Doordarshan, it's the government's job to point out each and every flaw of national life. It's Rajani's mission to confront, battle and defeat each and every flaw, and it's the job of the opposition and intellectuals to celebrate and applaud Rajani.

What a strange creation Rajani is! Without a sword or a horse, she's exactly like an avatar of Kalki. Armed with no more than a murderous glance and sharp tongue, she is able to defeat each and every type of wickedness. After meeting her, police officers, drug dealers and education board members follow her every step, wagging their tails behind them. Seeing Rajani's success, why shouldn't we request her to complete some other difficult tasks?

Such as . . .

FIRST EPISODE: Stop things from spinning so much in the evening. Rajani's sidekick, meaning, her husband, and she go to the 'Western' liquor store to buy a bottle of whiskey. There, she meets twenty or so corpses on the ground. She discovers that their deaths were caused by the toxic counterfeit liquor sold at the shop. Right then and there,

Rajani incites a revolution against the sale of counterfeit liquor, and the people come to her support. Someone whistles for the intersection's traffic cop to come over—he's to come arrest the shopkeeper! But, even before that, the shopkeeper falls at Rajani's feet, praises her and begs for her forgiveness. Rajani wrings a promise from him that he will sell only real liquor from then on, and she forgives him. But she says, 'For these murders, you'll still have to go to jail.' The shopkeeper replies, 'Don't worry. As soon as you pour some top-quality liquor in their throats, they'll spring back to life.'

SECOND EPISODE: A bloodthirsty gangster's gang is attacking a marketplace. They take a hefty chunk of change out of the monthly income of the restaurant, the cinema, the shops and so on, and they take a cut from even the notoriously corrupt doctor. Whoever refuses has their ears and nose cut off. On the urgent request of one hotel owner, Rajani builds up her fury and meets a minister of parliament. Disgusted with his sliminess, she goes to the Inspector General of Police. He tells her that the head of the mafia received a bribe from the politician, and she sets off to get the politician. The minister of parliament evades the issue. As soon as Rajani says that she's not any old Rajani, she's actually Priya Tendulkar just come from the prime minister and about to go back to tell him everything about him, the minister gets worried and calls the mafia don. As soon as the don arrives, he joins hands with Rajani and pledges to abjure violence. He promises her, 'Dear sister, from now on, I'll take the money of the shopkeepers with the same love and deep feelings that our party takes election donations from factory owners.'

THIRD EPISODE: As soon as our prime minister reads his speech about the country's opposition to Israel's bombing of the PLO camp in Tunisia, Rajani first heads off to America to talk to President Reagan. She scolds him. But, disappointed in him, she goes to India's famous police officer and Gujarat's Director General of Police Ribeiro and devises a plan to go with him to meet the prime minister of Israel. Ribeiro gives the suggestion of taking along the Punjab governor, Arjun Singh, who has had such wonderful success against terrorists.

In this episode, Rajani accomplishes a complete and sterling diplomatic defeat of Israel. How exactly this will happen I leave to 'Rajani's' beloved director, Basu Chatterjee.

13

Government's Beautiful Dream

Aside from a few incidents during exams, there's no cheating in high school and intermediate college. The real fraud is the fake news being spread by the opposition party ...

This was the drift of what the Uttar Pradesh Education Minister said several days ago at the Upper State House. And you might not believe this, but she was a teacher and a principal herself!

The gist of what the honorable education minister said, or wanted to say, was the following: Two million students take their final high school and intermediate exams each year. At most 20,000 students copy, or are caught cheating. So, out of all the test takers, the cheaters barely register one per cent! Which is nothing. That's not really cheating, is it? I don't think so.

It's the same as the fake news spread by the opposition and the media about rape. It's said that, last year, Uttar

Pradesh had the honor of having the most rapes of any Indian state. About 1500 incidents were reported to the police. The home minister, another honorable woman, could use the logic of the education minister, if she wanted. In Uttar Pradesh, there are more than 55 million women. Take away those under the age of eleven and those over 55, and there are about 30 million women at the risk of rape. Out of those, 1500 rape victims are merely 0.0002 per cent. That's the same thing as not happening!

In short, when you spin the government statistics, what you come up with is that everything is fine under the heavens, and Vishnu is resting peacefully on Shesh Shaiya at the bottom of the sea.

But now let's leave behind the air-conditioned world of the spin rooms and the brown-nosers of the education minister and return to the unflattering reality. Go to any high school or intermediate test centre. There's no need to go far. Go to places around the capital, like Intauja, Gosainganj, Mohanlal Ganj, Nigoha or next to the army base, Telibagh, famous for moonshine and smuggling.

But before we dive into the scene in question, we must understand three words in the dialect of our sect of copycats: (1) 'ward' or 'candidate', meaning the boy or girl at the test centre whom a bodyguard, police officer, police chief, teacher, politician or thug clearly points out so as to indicate to the centre administrator or test proctor whom to allow to cheat; (2) the 'matter', meaning a book, its ripped cover, some paper or some other item onto which the test answers can be copied; and (3) 'henchman'—this half-obscene word expresses the committed police officer, soldier, test proctor, etc., this person's complete and utter devotion to a child, and how they will relinquish all self-respect to do anything in order for the child to pass.

Now, if the test is to start at seven in the morning, then, at the test centre, the test sheets are opened at half past six. A copy of the test appears immediately at some building 200 metres away where two 'scholars' are quickly making a master cheat sheet. It's all done in under an hour. They fold up the answer sheet. This is the 'matter'. Dozens of people have been waiting to get the matter for their 'ward'. Rubber bands make this easier. After you put a rubber band around the matter, if you want, you can even write the name of your ward. If not, it's enough to write 'classroom #7, seat #19'. In exchange for the matter, what you give the scholar isn't a bribe or a fee, it's 'reimbursement for services rendered'.

Inside, the kids have been hard at work for an hour. Outside, a motorcycle is parked underneath a tamarind tree. It's a classic make—a Rajdoot or a Royal Enfield. It belongs to the police chief who is returning home from work. After having tea, he has come to the test centre out of a sense of duty, or because of the henchmen. There are already two or three police officers present, and two or three times as many bodyguards. Everyone is involved in something: either as a henchman, in the scheme of 'services rendered', or in tea-and-samosa bribery, all for the sake of their ward, or the ward of a friend or family member, or the ward of a well-wisher.

The test-takers have already ripped the covers off their books or notebooks and put them in their pockets. Or stuffed them in their pants. Or secured them to their drawstrings. Or cosseted them in the hidden mountain pass in their bosom. They have already taken their seats and begun the work at hand. Then, to distribute the matter, the cheat sheets—duplicated through carbon copying or through professional photocopying in town—reach the test centres.

When one bodyguard can't find class #7, seat #19, he curses under his breath: *how the fuck are these seats arranged?!* The test proctor comes over, asks what he's looking for.

'Which one is seat #19?'

A skinny girl raises her hand. The bodyguard slips the folded matter onto her lap.

Then the police chief strides in.

'How are things going, Master Sahib?' he asks. The test proctor smiles broadly. This is his life's crowning glory. From this day on, the police captain will know who he is. Now anytime he wants, he can get his neighbor charged with IPC #107, aiding and abetting.

The police captain answers the test proctor's insinuating look with a question, 'This is class #6, right? Where's seat #14?'

The test proctor extends his hand and takes the matter, saying, 'Please let me handle it. You'll get lost looking for class #6.'

He goes to class #6.

'How's it going?' the class #6 test proctor asks the class #7 test proctor.

The class #7 proctor makes a face. He looks like he's swallowing bile. Then he says, 'It's hell.'

He drops the matter onto seat #14, then returns to his colleague. He says, 'I've half a mind to resign. This fucking government . . .' It's like he was sent to earth to become Swami Vivekananda, but the fucking government has turned him into Haji Mastan.

On his rounds, the centre administrator comes to class #7. A handful of boys are copying straight from books.

'What's going on, Master Sahib?' he asks.

'It's hell, sir!' the class #7 proctor says. 'I've confiscated and burned cheat sheets five times already! But one of them always takes out something else, and it starts up again!'

In a holy rage, the centre administrator asks for all the matter to be tossed out the window. Then he starts off in the direction of the tamarind tree to go chat with the police captain. Just then, from near the front gate, a ruckus can be heard: *ho ho, hee hee, hoo hoo, ho ho!* The class proctor suddenly climbs onto his chair. The test-takers take out matter from desks, pockets, depths of blouses and ends of pant drawstrings. They throw them out the windows into the backyard. The college servants, sweepers and some zealous guardians hurry to fill gunnysacks with the matter and hide the gunnysacks from view. In the commotion, some Nirodh condom packets are exchanged, as well as bills and loose change. In the chaos, the test proctor gathers up whatever matter falls onto the classroom floor with his own two hands and throws it out the window.

So what ends up happening? Rajdoot and Royal Enfields are old and out of date; the police captain rides them. These days, it's Suzukis or Hero Hondas that are all the rage, and many are already parked near the front gate, with their accompanying guardians. A couple of guardians are stationed as lookouts. They are two or three hundred metres from the test centre, staring down the route where at any moment the inspection team will sweep in: a jeep carrying the assistant director along with the zila college superintendent or the team of the deputy of elementary education. As soon as the jeep's hood is sighted in the distance, the lookouts hammer the accelerators on their Suzukis or Hero Hondas and speed toward the test centre at 80 kilometres an hour. Upon their signal, the guardians parked at the gate and the hangers-on eating samosas and drinking tea shout at the top of their lungs in an animal-like language. Immediately, the entire test centre begins to throw out gunnysacks filled with matter to the dozens of men waiting outside to welcome the inspection team.

In this commotion, some matter belonging to some wards falls on the desks, beneath the chairs, or at the feet of other wards. These wards will be caught and charged, and the authorities will proceed with the necessary measures. There are also those test-takers who have entirely forgotten about things such as matter, and they still have cheat sheets in their pockets. They are caught.

When the honorable education minister mentioned the 20,000 cheaters in her speech, most are these unfortunate souls.

14

Great Painter, Bad Critic

Professor Pannalal was once the famous backdrop painter for the Nishat Theatrical Company. Once upon a time, people would travel from Bombay to Calcutta to see his painted backdrops, and if the theater company was performing in Bombay, then people would travel from Calcutta to Bombay. And such beautiful backdrops they were! There, a red sun rises over black mountains, puffy white clouds float above the green jungle, and, here, in the foothills, a river flows, a white ghat can be seen, beautiful women are bathing, the water is blue. (And that's not even to mention how the water reflects the beauty of the clouds!) There, on the dirt road, there are two gentlemen strolling along, wearing sports coats, Western pants, they have big mustaches and walking canes, they are out because, as I just mentioned, morning is a wonderful time of day, in other words, there are women bathing nearby.

But now those sets are no more. Cinema has replaced the theater, and, in place of professional theater companies, there are student productions in schools and colleges that, because they have no funding, have to act out what the set used to show. So, the professor is now retired. He stays at home to paint. His paintings are known for their profusion of riverbanks, palm trees, bathing girls, full moons and rising suns. These paintings are priced from eight annas to eight rupees. Since Professor Sahib is good at his craft, there's no worry about keeping food on his table. These paintings have become very popular in town, and you can even find them hung cut along the backs of the stalls of tobacco and betel-nut vendors.

In these circumstances, it's natural that after a long career as a respected artist, Professor Pannalal would also become an art critic. Occasionally, when he comes over to pay me a visit, he offers a little modern art critique. Referring to modern art, he says, 'Beauty is in the eye of the beholder.'

Yesterday, as soon as he came, he asked, 'So, who's this Jamini Roy? At the Imperial Company, they had some Roy or Rai. Is that him?'

'No, that's not possible,' I said, respectfully. 'Jamini Roy is Bengali.'

'Same as the other one! It's possible they're related.'

It didn't seem at all likely that Jamini Roy had any connection to the backdrop painter for the Imperial Company. So, I shook my head vigorously, 'No, Jamini Roy's no relation to him.'

Professor Pannalal came right up to my side, sat down, and said, 'So, my friend, I went to Delhi. I went to an art show, and everywhere I looked, it was Jamini Roy. I had to avert my eyes and flee. I'm an artist, after all, my friend, and if I see something awful, that's what will come out when I'm painting.'

'They were that ugly?' I asked, surprised.

He got even more upset. 'Ugly? My friend, ugly and beautiful, these are words we use for describing real paintings . . .'

'Professor Sahib,' I interrupted him in a very learned tone. 'Tell me more about Jamini Roy. What was missing from his art, in your opinion?'

'Look here, my friend,' he replied. 'I can't talk about what's missing. We all live through our talents. Someday, when Jamini Roy makes some paintings, then we'll talk about what's missing. But when will that be? He makes artless sketches of elephants, horses and soldiers. They look like what village women make to decorate their doors. If you call that painting, then what are my paintings?'

'Professor Sahib,' I began to explain. 'Jamini Roy draws deep inspiration from lokjivan, from folklore, and . . .'

But now there was no holding him back. He said, 'Oh, Lokjivan! Yes, he could be an artist. He must be the brother of the Mahabali Company's Harjivan. But speaking of Harjivan, what's he good at?'

What could I say?

Content with his victory, he spoke to defeated me in a generous, calm tone, 'Look here, we're not talking about folklore or Harjivan. We're talking about Jamini Roy. I remember one of his paintings called "Black Horse". What should I say? It had only one eye, and it was as round as a gooseberry. Its legs were like upturned maces or bowling pins, its tail was like the crest of a Jodphuri turban and its ears were like a donkey's. Instead of a saddle, there was a rug flung over its back, and instead of stirrups, there was a bell on one side. So, no stirrups, no saddle, no reins, and yet there's this black horse all ready to go?'

I changed my argument's tack. 'But, Professor, you remember it in such great detail! How else could you have remembered the black horse's bell?'

Now, he was revved up. 'It wasn't just that one,' he said. 'I saw his other paintings too. In one, there were some girlsish faces passed off as five sisters. Their faces were identical. It was hard to say what kind of creature had spawned them! I have to tell you, I have painted life-size portraits of women. I'm talking about one backdrop. When women drew close to it, one-third fainted, one-third clutched their heads and sighed and one-third started reciting ghazals! But, here, the figures were so generic—it was like all women on earth are sisters. Anyway, enough of this Jamini Roy!'

I didn't try to contradict him, but in order to redeem Jamini Roy, I said, 'And were there other paintings? Some more must have been sent from Calcutta.'

'Don't ask about any others!' Professor Pannalal said, screwing up his nose. 'It's a sign of the times. Everything's fast and splashy. It's all loud and gaudy.' He fell silent. Then suddenly he began again, 'There was Abanindranath Tagore, Nandalal, Sharda Vakil, Haldar, Majumdar—so many painters heaped together. But they were all the same! I couldn't stand them!'

'What was wrong with them?'

'When the whole world worships these paintings, who am I to say anything? But their eyes are too big for their faces, and their fingers are too big for their hands. I'm sorry, my friend, but where on earth do people look like this?' For half a minute, he was a picture of tranquility. Then he started up again, hot and heavy, 'It would be wrong to call them paintings, but what else can you call them? Nandalal Sahib has one painting called "Spring". Now ask me what's meant by the word "spring". Spring is when trees and bushes are thick with blooms, when the air is light and heady, when koels sing, when bees buzz and when separated lovers wander through gardens cursing the god of love. So, this is spring, but ask Nandalal Sahib if he knows this. In this one painting, it's just three trees. It's desolate. Something's on the branches—leaves or flowers, it's impossible to say. Two people are fleeing, and two others holding torches are giving chase. It looks like one is a pregnant woman. So, a baby suggests spring. But that's it for spring, my friends— no heady breeze, no koel, no separated lovers!'

Professor Pannalal laughed. Hearing his boisterous, spiteful laugh, I asked, 'So, you don't like Bengali painters. You must have seen some paintings from Bombay, too.'

This incited him. 'Please don't mention them. I've lived in Bombay. Once upon a time, people there could admire my paintings, but now they have to suffer through this! It's horrible! So, in one, there are three very black women sitting down. It's by Chavda. It looks like one woman is grinding something in a mortar. There's not much to it. There are some fish flopping around and a water pot.

But it's not clear what the shapes are. And they call this a painting? Now it's all like this.'

'This is the Progressives.'

He furrowed his brow. 'It's like someone said, "Just make a triangle" or "sketch a square" or "put an eye in the middle of some weeds" or "make a head but no feet" or "make some feet, but only feet and more feet". That's what you mean, right? Their naivety is supposed to be enough to compete with the West, you think?'

Once he mentioned the West, I said, 'Stop for a moment. Amrita Sher-Gil has shown paintings in France and has done very well for herself.'

'So what? I've seen her paintings. Compared to Jamini Roy's, if you look at the figures, you can actually tell they're sisters. But, if you look at them up close, it's hard to say who's the older one, who's the younger one, who's married and who's not. Who in the West is going to come calling for that? A painting should be a painting. But, these days, you can call anything a painting. In one, you have a room where there are some teacups here and there on a table. Now, sir, a certain man told me that even if there are no people present, it looks like people were there, drank tea, then left. I said, "But, my friend, what proof is there? It looks to me that the servant has clumsily set out the tea, and people are on their way to the table." It's whatever you want it to be!'

'But even if there was proof, so what?' I asked.

'Aren't some things just real in the way they are? Now you have to think about everything!'

I felt the last drops of my patience being wrung from my body. 'Professor!' I said. 'The fact is that you don't know anything about modern art! To understand it, you have to use your mind as well as your eyes.'

But Professor Pannalal was ready for this, as well. He smiled, and, without saying anything, he said that this was just the sort of thing he expected from the young men of my generation. 'Okay, okay,' he said. 'That's something that artists of my times never said. We're backward in that way. You people sing in a roundabout way. If you don't like the song, you don't blame the singer, you blame the person listening. If you like an English song that makes a tarana seem old and stodgy, if we say we don't like it, you say the older generation doesn't understand anything. It's the same in art. The painting is right there in front of us, I'm looking at it, and I don't like it. It's not a goddess, a god, a man, a woman, a scene depicting nature's beauty or human wisdom. It's just a twisted mess. I look at it and say it's worthless, and you say I don't get it. I mean, I'm staring at the painting, and you say I'm not looking at it!'

Maybe Professor Pannalal was going to call witnesses. So, I said, 'But these paintings have won all sorts of prizes . . .'

'Prizes? The government gives prizes to classical songs and to film songs, to literary books and to mass-market books. It's the same in every genre of art. It's only painting that gets people confused! I was just about to say that when you give prizes to paintings that have five misaligned circles for eyes, then show a little love for my paintings of religious, traditional scenes. Moony eyes are good for moony rooms, but paintings of religious, traditional scenes are in each and every ordinary person's house! Please think of these too!'

It took him a while to calm down. Then, suddenly, he laughed, as though he had remembered something. 'My friend,' he began. 'They say it's mass-rule, democracy, and we're artists for the masses. How dumb do you look when you laugh at us now?'

He put his hand on his chest and laughed so that his mustache wiggled and stretched, and then I was certain that Professor Pannalal wasn't just the backdrop painter for the Nishat Theatrical Company, but that he had also ventured onto the stage itself. I accepted my ignorance and begged his forgiveness. He forgave me and praised the modesty of my upbringing.

15

White-Collar Revolution

The white-collar revolution, I mean the bellicose attitude of ordinary people, I mean middle-class militancy, isn't fueled only by inflation and rising expenses. Behind it, there's also the competition to buy social advantages, personal benefits and everything that makes life more convenient, which leads the white-collar worker to spend money wildly and to cry non-stop about their destitution.

Imagine that you're a foreigner (which isn't hard to do because most English-speaking Indians consider themselves foreigners), and that you've just come to India, and that you're sitting in the lounge of a five-star hotel flipping through the pages of a magazine like *Illustrated Weekly* or *Femina*. Reading the ads, you'll start thinking like this: India's poverty has been wiped away . . . India is once again the golden bird . . . India is born from the 'Pride of Femininity' B.C.N. saris . . . with Indian Fish-brand razors, a man is always in control . . . in India Chandela was all the rage (a new color, a new design, every day) . . . in India, wearing

Tombray Dying clothes, you'll have the confidence to look right into the camera and everyone will look at you (or at least at the five young ladies in the picture) . . . India's Sipton tea is second to none . . . for India's new generation, Siviya cream . . . brush with Binaca toothpaste and young ladies the world over will welcome your kisses . . . eat Tanasin, strum your sitar, then take your lover out for a picnic . . .

If you're really middle-class, buy all of these things! Eat all of these products! Cry about your cash-flow problems day and night! Shout at the top of your lungs the slogans of the revolution!

And the pictures of the high life and the life of leisure that these ads present aren't entirely false. They suggest that inside India there's another India, white-collar India, which is crammed full of the products of consumerism. Everything is available: from British razor blades to Japanese tape recorders, from toasters to electric ranges and televisions, from whisky to Hadensa hemorrhoid cream. Parisian jewelry and Japanese saris are part of this world, though it's another matter that Japanese women don't wear saris.

Being able to purchase these things is what motivates the white-collar, middle-class revolutionaries; it's what gets them to shout slogans, to demonstrate in the streets, to go to jail over their demand for a one-hundred-rupee raise.

Manual laborers and the poor also shout slogans, demonstrate in the streets and go to jail and get shot for it. But their revolution and the white-collar revolution are different. Their revolution puts in doubt the survival of the administrative class; they want to buck the system. Under the banner of their revolution, white-collar workers want to protect the establishment. Instead of getting rid of the system, they try to get more concessions to strengthen their hold on things. That is, when engineers, doctors, civil servants and so on are on the warpath, I don't get too worried. I know they're the sorts of donkeys that make a fuss when they're in the stable, but, once they get out and stretch their legs a bit, they're more than happy to escort themselves back to the barn and close the door behind them.

There's no big decision that has to be made to pacify the white-collar revolution. It's enough to replace one title with another: 'junior engineer' instead of 'overseer'. Their goals are quite small. Whether they say it or not, the goals of their revolution are to get a refrigerator to replace the ice box, to send their girls to the Loreto Convent instead of the Lalita Rani Balika Vidyalaya, to buy Black Dog whisky instead of Black Knight beer and to use the word 'rodent' to refer to the animal instead of the word 'rat'. All in all, their food and drink, as well as their lifestyle, should reach the level being promoted so evocatively in the ads in *Illustrated* and *Femina*.

There's one more difference between the revolutions of white-collar and dirty-collar workers. Dirty-collar workers demand equality, while the attitude of white-collar workers follows this quote by George Orwell: 'All animals are equal, but some animals are more equal.'

So, when IAS officers are on the warpath, they have two demands: (1) they shouldn't be thought of as a tiger or a cheetah but as a lion, the king of the jungle, and (2) everyone else should be considered a jackal.

The engineer says that he won't accept being called a big fat elephant. He wants to be thought of as a lion, like IAS officers, on the condition that PCS officers shouldn't be given any more status than the leopard, or, at most, the cheetah. When the doctor steps out of his lair-cum-private-practice-clinic, he asks to be thought of as no worse than a tiger, and that other civil servants be bears, adaptable to living on the ground or in trees. The instructor at a degree-granting college wants others to think of him as an Arabian stallion and nothing less, while high school and intercollege instructors should be considered asses. The lawyers arguing at the Lucknow High Court don't argue with the lawyers of the Allahabad High Court about who's above whom—they're both bulls and remain so. But the Lucknavi lawyer revolts; he wants to increase the acreage of his pastures.

And so this whole revolution, this rebellion, resembles a dirty pond whose little waves dash against one another, stridently undercutting one another, and the lush trees and greenery lining the pond is in no danger at all.

Reading this, you might think that I don't feel the pain of white-collar workers. For the last twenty-five years, I've been carrying the burden of a white collar around my neck, and I understand their neck pain as much as I do my own. But I also know that this pain is usually related to ads that make you want to buy things for birthdays, weddings and dowries, or to buy things to make your life more convenient. These can be grouped under the label of inflation and rising expenses. But if they didn't exist, the pain would still be there because the white-collar worker

16

Mummyji's Donkey

One

In the arcanum of world geography, there is a tehsil called Bansgaon whose residents long ago spread across the globe from Trinidad to Bangkok and who are famous for their knowledge and ignorance, a little more for the former than the latter. Wherever they live, they have made a name for themselves. For those who don't know world geography, Bansgaon is in the Gorakhpur district of Uttar Pradesh. Our donkey, I mean, our hero, was born there.

Mannan Dwivedi Gajpuri, the famous poet, was from Bansgaon. He has one poem that goes like this:

> There was a fat, ornery donkey
> That thought he was king of the jungle
> If he ever found a lion's pelt
> There'd be no convincing him he wasn't

At the beginning of this century, when Hindi criticism was yet unaware of the concept of plainspokenness, many people must have seen in this children's verse both plainspokenness and a Panchatantra tale's moral. But, as this story will prove, there's neither plainspokenness nor moral in this poem—just as there's none in Indian history and in George Orwell's *1984*. In today's poetry, if the donkey gets up and leaves, it's not coming back. Led on by hooliganism, political infighting, the power of a money or an injunction issued by the Supreme Court, the donkey, even if the lion's pelt slides off its back, continues to sit in front of our door and growl, exactly like a tiger.

In any event, there's no need to get into all of that. This is simply the story of my son, whom we used to affectionately call our 'donkey'. While this could be the story of anyone's son, but since most would rather not admit how my son's story resembles that of their own, I've limited this story to the events of our donkey's life.

Two

When my son was a boy, my wife and I—enamored with some of his qualities—gave him the nickname 'donkey'. He was stubborn, slow and fond of singing loudly without any forewarning at all. He wouldn't run far away and hide after being spanked. He liked being one of a group, but he liked being alone even more. He was actually born in April and so lived up to the Sanskrit word for donkey, which translates to 'born in April'. Like donkeys, he was sad during the monsoon and happy in the summer. But this wasn't for the same reason as donkeys. There were other reasons. The reason was that he was often sick during the monsoons, and he would go with his mom to Nainital or Ranikhet to enjoy the pleasant summer weather.

Our donkey, like other donkeys, loved to sing, and he sang well. When our friends and neighbors wanted to make us feel good, they would mention his singing. Neighbors would go out for their evening stroll and come pay us a visit (both to waste time and to be friendly). As soon as they sat down, we would serve them tea, cookies, soft drinks and so on to fulfill our duty as hosts and to get them to leave as soon as possible. Then, we would quickly present our boy so that they could ask him to sing a song, and, after hearing our son, they could sing his praises to his face and to his parents' faces. Then, seeing how there was nothing more to do at our house and thinking that they should do as they had first planned and go out for that evening walk, they would leave.

On one such evening, struck by an impulse to be super friendly, one visitor said, 'My boy, my donkey, sing a song, would you?'

At the time, our boy was four years old. He got upset. He said, 'Don't call me "donkey". I'm not your donkey, I'm only Mummyji's donkey!'

Three

It's hard to imagine, but what our donkey said then has become a guiding principle of Indian politics—a 'directive principle'—twenty-five years later.

'Ingrate,' our guest whispered, so softly that I could barely hear him, yet loud enough so that I would definitely hear him. Then, laughing, he turned to leave, 'I have to get home for a guest who's on his way.'

And he left.

It's hard to imagine, but what our guest said then has also become a guiding principle of Indian politics twenty-five years later.

Four

My wife was very pleased with our guest's accusation. She liked to read the newspaper. Every day, she read the crafty and disrespectful words of thousands of well-educated and respectable public leaders and so had already decided that my son shouldn't be just a donkey, but rude as well. So, we spent money hand over fist on his education, gave him a first-rate education and forced him abroad to a get an advanced technical degree. When he returned, our donkey even became a sharp-tongued member of the state electricity board.

He was rude and insulting, and he started to become famous. And so, he quickly started to become beloved among his peers. The reverence others had for him grew further when, as soon as he got his job, he started a revolution: an upper-class revolution, by the upper classes, for the upper classes, a revolution called 'the generalists versus the specialists', or the revolution of 'the ordinary bureaucrats versus the specialists'. Our son unleashed the rallying cry that the generalists should be forced out from his organization—those generalists, the last vestiges of British rule, were occupying important positions, thanks to a nationwide conspiracy. As youthful blood remains at a constant boil in every revolution, all the young officers joined, and, in calling for the removal of the old guard, they shouted things like 'pull 'em by the ear', 'shove 'em out' and 'wrangle 'em by the neck', or whatever idioms were customary within their local dialects and cultural norms. The revolution picked up steam, and the rude and disrespectful words of well-educated and respectable public leaders on both sides of the debate ignited newspapers and infatuated coffee houses. Government in-fighting turned into public out-fighting.

One day, I seized the chance in front of me; I mean, I saw him singing to himself, and I said, 'Look, son, what are you all mixed up in now?' (I no longer called him 'donkey') 'It's not about the generalists or specialists. No position should be reserved for anyone. Whether a generalist or a specialist, the best person for the job should get the job.'

'This is exactly what the generalists say!' my son said. 'They've used this against us for years, turned us into fools just to drag us around by the nose, while they're living it up! The people . . .'

'Son, don't talk about "the people". "The people" mention you all in the same breath. You all steal money with both hands, you all profiteer to advance your careers, you all take advantage of them, you all live in the same type of fancy bungalow, you all drive the same type of car . . .'

'Papa, it's really hard to understand what you're saying,' my son said. 'If we lived in the same type of bungalow, if we used the same type of car, if everything was the same, then why don't the people elect the district magistrate to be their MLA, and the MLA to be their district magistrate?'

Five

And so, the revolution was our son's first accomplishment upon becoming a high-ranking bureaucrat. His second accomplishment was learning bridge, billiards, table tennis, dancing, painting and other leisure activities and arts, as was standard. (Up until then, he had only learned music.) At the same time as his generalist-versus-specialist revolution gained momentum, he followed in the long tradition of high-ranking bureaucrats by putting his newfound knowledge to work and offer his unsolicited opinions about writers, poets, political leaders, philosophers, social reformers, scientists, journalists, etc., etc., etc. One day, he announced that he wasn't ideologically opposed to the prime minister; he agreed with him that Indian journalists weren't to be trusted. That very day, journalists ran very colorful stories about his comments, and a large photo accompanied the articles. My own observation was that his personal relationships with journalists grew only stronger, for however much he denounced them en masse. So much about my son remained outside of my comprehension!

Then, his third and largest accomplishment was his sudden hatred for water buffalos, pigs and donkeys.

Six

These days, water buffalos, pigs and donkeys have attained a special status in the life of the city, so much so that there's nothing more that really needs to be said about them. In short, for the last twenty or twenty-five years, especially from the time that heavy-handed administrators took over city councils and municipal committees (and so what was 'local autonomous government' stopped being 'local' 'autonomous' and 'government'), herds of water buffalos, drifts of pigs and droves of donkeys became symbols of the city. In the Bhagavad Gita, the sort of objectivity defined there considers a learned Brahmin, a cow, an elephant, a dog and a Chandal as equals. Now, this is the guiding philosophy of the majority of city managers. And so, the water buffalo pokes its horns into the pants of the traffic cop standing at the intersection, and donkeys gallop down the street in front of the scooters like a military escort leading the governor's car. Water buffalos, pigs and donkeys are everywhere—in the very best neighborhoods, on the streets, in beautiful parks, in tight alleys, up to the gates of elegant bungalows. City administrators now follow the social philosophy that everyone has the right to live anywhere and side by side with everyone else, and their implementation strategy is that if you can't raise the poor to the level of the rich, then you can cut down the rich to the level of the poor. They have read the handbook for city development whose first lesson goes like this:

CITY: a pigsty with water buffalo stables

RELIGIOUS CITY: a city in the middle of a donkey stable with a seven-day-old Santoshi Mata or a Hanumanji temple at some random intersection

SECULAR CITY: a religious city with a five-day-old Muslim saint's shrine located somewhere or other.

Anyway, it should be clear that the people to blame are not the water buffalo, pig or donkey owners; if there's fault to be found, it's the fault of those who don't own water buffalos, pigs or donkeys. Because these days you can't get by in the city without them!

There's some Ayurvedic scholar going by the name of Charak who has filled the minds of Indians with his inexhaustible reverence for raw milk. (There are so many Charaks, but there's one in particular I'm talking about.) We've renounced milk bottled in factories, and when we set out for the buffalo stables with our buckets dangling, the 'cult' of water buffalos grows with our every step. A water buffalo tied to a stake can give you milk either in a park filled with buffalo pee, buffalo poop and mud (a park that the water buffalo herders must have just 'freed' from the city administrators' beautification projects), or along a wide street in Civil Lines. From raw milk, you get energy, knowledge, wisdom, longevity and so on. Those who aren't vegetarians justify pigs in a similar way. And both vegetarians and non-vegetarians can justify donkeys.

Well, especially donkeys. Because wherever there are white-collar workers, there are washermen, and wherever there's a washerman, there's a donkey, and, as the ranks of white-collar workers grow and their neighborhoods expand, the numbers of city water buffalos, pigs and especially donkeys grow just as fast.

Seven

Sociology sidetracked me. Now, back to the main story.

Our son spent several years in West Germany, then returned to become an official on the state electricity board. He lived in a big bungalow in a newly built neighborhood. After getting back from West Germany, for a couple of days he complained incessantly about the crowds in the streets, the bad drivers, the claustrophobic telephone booths and the paan stalls. Then he turned to complain about the spiritual and physical health of Indians, or their absence. He said, 'Even when they laugh, they're not happy. On the street or at the office, at the store or at home, they look bitter, spent, unhinged. Or, if not that, then just depressed.'

I suggested that he go to any one of the new hotels where the youth go for disco dancing and drinking liquor and where they look so happy that it's like they're the young men and women in Doordarshan commercials—the girls are sipping soft drinks and the guys are splashing in the ocean or riding motorcycles like they're airplanes. Sucking hand-size bottles of flavored water, they're exemplars of health, beauty and freedom—which are the lofty promises of Pick-up Cola or Pepsi Cola. But my son turned up his nose at this too, saying, 'Papa, watching these four-foot-eleven-and-a-half-inch girls and guys as skinny as scarecrows dance makes me feel sorry for my country.

If you made them run 500 metres, they'd faint. They need fruit juice and vitamins.'

Even in the speeches of the Twenty-Point Program people, I hadn't heard about the bad physical health of our youth. And on Doordarshan there was no shortage of shows featuring the liberated, crazy dancing of the youth, so I didn't agree with my son's depressing conclusion. But he was six-feet tall and had a sturdy physique, which all the food and drink in Germany had accentuated, so I didn't raise any objections. But I understood his point: above all else, he didn't want to see any sign of ugliness, weakness or clumsiness at home. And so, in short order, his house became a showcase for beauty, finery, music, art, etc., etc., etc. I mean, it became a capitalist, consumerist, posh bourgeois playhouse. So, for however much ungainliness, decay and weakness he saw outside, inside his other India, he could easily forget the one outside. Immediately inside his gate, there were all types of trees, vines, creepers, flowers and bushes, as well as a perfectly manicured lawn and beautiful garden paths. Once inside the living room, there were pots of sweet-smelling, verdant house plants, pieces of art hung on the walls, expensive hand-woven carpets on the floor and Ravi Shankar or Western music coming from hidden speakers.

It was another matter that outside the gate, pigs roamed the streets snorting loudly, donkeys hee-hawed raucously and water buffalos were absolutely everywhere, while trucks honked in arpeggios, scooters tweeted apologetically, rickshaws chirped and chirruped and the life of the city dissolved in a sea of confusion.

Eight

Then a donkey entered the gate.

When the donkey entered, my son was in his bedroom correcting a presentation document whose papers were spread over his rug. This 171-page document had to be given to the chief minister in two days, and through its countless arguments, projections, theoretical considerations, historical anecdotes and analytical examples, it requested that a technical specialist (instead of an ordinary bureaucrat) be placed at the head of the Secretariat's electricity ministry. Since I was once an ordinary bureaucrat, my son launched into his points with a special fervor. And since I knew my son's commitment, had no such commitment myself and had a long time ago read the story of Tweedledee and Tweedledum, I avoided speaking about the hidden challenges facing my son. I listened to his entire presentation, and I didn't naysay a single thing. In any event, my son was in his bedroom, and I was in the living room when we heard the deafening noise of a donkey's full-throated, spontaneous braying.

The gardener's little boy was on the lawn doing some work. He must not have seen the donkey come in, or if he had seen it, he must have thought it wasn't anything out of the ordinary. Hearing the explosive braying, I froze for a second, then leaped into motion and went out to the verandah. My son arrived from the opposite direction at just the same time. He was yelling at the top of his lungs. Hearing him, the gardener and his little boy sprang toward the donkey.

The donkey was nibbling on a rare Brazilian plant. The gardener and his son raced up to the donkey. When they got there, they realized they were empty-handed. Still screaming, my son picked up an empty pot and threw it at the donkey's back. It—I mean, the pot—broke into pieces. One shard hit the gardener, who was bending down to pick up a shovel from the lawn, in the back. The gardener shot up, turned around, and looked at the donkey, as though the pot had been broken across his back and not the donkey's. With the shovel in hand, he sprung forward to scare off the donkey.

But that wasn't necessary. The donkey had already run away, although it's another matter that it didn't head for the gate but went first to the lawn. The donkey advanced slowly, but it eventually picked up its tail and galloped away. Then, with shouting and screaming coming from every direction, it got frightened and started cutting shapes into the lawn—a circle, a triangle, then a square. It ran roughshod over several bushes, broke some pots and, without being able to make out one direction from another, actually chose the right direction, that is, the one leading to the front gate. It slipped through and raced away.

Nine

Afterward, the donkey became a frequent visitor. It seemed that whenever the gate was left open just a bit, it would slip in. It had taken a particular liking to the Brazilian bush. If the donkey wasn't immediately beaten out of the yard, it wouldn't touch any plant other than the 'foreign goods', toward which it would inch with real devotion. Even when beaten with a stick, it would only reluctantly turn back and leave through the gate. And now there wasn't a big hue and cry every time it entered: after the first time, the donkey had stopped announcing its entrance with loud braying. And my son wasn't always around either to shout at the top of his lungs. Now the ritual was strictly between the gardener and the donkey. The donkey would enter, and the gardener would beat it away.

But, for my son, it wasn't just the problem of a stray donkey. It wasn't limited either to the fact that it put the flowers and plants in danger. When it came through the gates to attack the bungalow, it also attacked our son's calm, his artistic feelings and his aesthetics. He scolded the gardener and one of the house servants, telling them to go complain to the donkey's owner that if he didn't tie it up, he would put a bullet through its head. But the donkey's owner never had the chance to act on this advice.

One day, hearing the gardener's yell, my son sprang up from his seat on the verandah. Despite suffering the blows of a gardener's stick, the donkey had latched onto the Brazilian plant and was thrashing it with its strong jaws. These guerrilla attacks were hard to put an end to, just like they are in Latin America. These were also the days when the generalists-versus-specialists debate was entering its final stage, and my son was going to take his delegation to visit the chief minister that evening. Whatever was the reason for his tense mood, my son went inside, came back with his rifle, and fired at the donkey as it trotted toward the gate, in flight after having just received a beating. The donkey collapsed in a heap. And so, a bridge was formed linking the street's depravity and the bungalow's exclusivity.

Ten

The owner found out about the donkey's death almost immediately. He came with several other men. The men with him started getting mad at my son. The donkey's owner was an old washerman. He had spent twenty-five years working at a British commissioner's bungalow. He was old now, and he had the vibe of a character from Rudyard Kipling. All he had to his name was his knowledge of a handful of English words, his courtesy and his donkey. While his friends started to get upset and my son was indifferent, the washerman remained patient. When he talked, he talked of his poverty and the horrors he had seen in his life. In the end, our son agreed to compensate the washerman for his donkey, and the amount they settled on was enough to please even the rabblerousers in the crowd.

But then our son's luck changed.

Suddenly, 150 or 200 people showed up at his bungalow. Their leader was a young man wearing a homespun bush shirt and pants who was shouting, 'Down with bureaucracy, down with bureaucracy!' The other people were screaming too. They were foaming at the mouth, spitting passion and anger and opposition and rebellion and revolution . . . all subjects were touched upon. All of the hullaballoo and the imprecations cast toward the police's spinelessness lasted for an hour. It was with great difficulty that the respectable washerman could get everyone to understand that 'the officer was willing to pay the price'.

'What fucking officer, and what fucking price?' someone said.

'You think this is some bus passenger struck by a bus and killed, and now his family has come to protest until they get their three thousand rupees?' someone else said.

Gradually, the police arrived, with armed reinforcements. Then more people came, and more after that. The news spread that one or two thousand people were surrounding the police station. Demands were made . . . *If he wasn't fired, if he wasn't arrested, if a case wasn't brought to trial, then the donkey's corpse would remain where it lay, no one would be allowed to remove it, the bungalow would be set afire and the police station would be stormed.* A little while later, the police captain and the collector left the police station for the bungalow, and, while walking back, they set to resolve the situation. They wanted to talk to the washerman, but the politician announced abruptly that he'd do the talking. The washerman's friends had already disappeared into the crowd. The washerman said that he was fine with whatever the politician said.

Eleven

To which party belonged the rabblerousing politician with his 'down with bureaucracy' anthems, his homespun bush shirt and pants? This was impossible to say because every fourth month he switched parties. At the time, he was sidling up to the ruling party, and that was the source of his power.

Yet, the source of his real power was land schemes, the beloved sideline of leaders like him. He wasn't so important that he could sell someone a platform at Patna Station or a university building in town, but he was certainly the type who knew when land was about to be bought for a new government housing colony, who would get there first, pay some bribes and put up some big housing developments. Sometimes, it also came to pass that the government would compensate a landowner for a soon-to-be-built government housing colony to be erected on his land, but instead of handing the land over, the landowner, with the politician's help, would sell the land to someone else. So, although having paid for the land, the government builders would show up to start building only to see Subhash Nagar already standing there!

Then, a couple days later, when the government men showed up at a second locale, there they found another development—Gandhi Nagar! Following this rubric, the politician had already built Ambedkar Nagar, Patel Nagar, Lohiya Nagar, Jawahar Nagar and Kamla Nagar. Since then, he'd moved on to the vihars. Developments were built on empty lots alongside roads. They were called Indra Vihar, Sanjay Vihar and Rajeev Vihar. Now, the politician was building for himself a big building with six-foot-wide storefronts and restaurants and whose upper floors would be occupied by a hotel. He was going to call the area Varun Vihar but switched to Sonia Vihar. All he would have to do was buy a new signboard.

The law that allowed these developments to be built was in a book that only politicians could access. Everyone used to ask how all of these developments—from Subhash Nagar to Varun (then Sonia) Vihar—could have been built without the permission of the municipal council, without asking the development authority and on the government housing council's land. But the answer could be found only in that special book. Be that as it may, the politician's answer was, 'Everything is for the people! What? Are you saying there's something illegal going on? So, go knock down Indira Vihar, go knock down Lohiya Nagar!'

Electricity was being pirated for these illegal housing developments, and that's where my son butted in. The issue of the electricity supply for 200 to 250 houses came up, and the politician demanded that if the city development authority gave him an electricity permit and legalized the development, then he would make these houses pay their bills. All the houses of Varun (or Sonia) Vihar were snared in this mess. My son wanted to take the law into his own hands to punish the politician, and now the dead donkey was being used as a cudgel against him.

The bureaucracy should be burned on the donkey's pyre . . . Its sparks should light the police station on fire . . . All day long, whatever else the conversation had been about, this is what the politician kept demanding. In the end, this is what ended up happening: our donkey—I mean, our son—paid compensation; a complaint about his action was filed at the police station; he was arrested; his bail couldn't be arranged; no judge could be found that evening to sign a bail bond, not at home, not in the market, not in the club, not in the pub; his gun was confiscated by the police; his license was revoked; the crowd that had gathered around the police station dispersed; the donkey's bier was loaded onto a truck with prayers and chants, then taken away for cremation; and, finally, the donkey's owner was left with an impossible future—with no donkey, and no means to earn a living.

Twelve

The next day, the newspapers ran the following headline: GENERALIST VERSUS SPECIALIST FIGHT TAKES NEW TURN. JOINT SECRETARY OF ELECTRICAL ENGINEERS UNION ARRESTED. ADMINISTRATIVE CONSPIRACY AFOOT. Now, I thought, top-level bureaucrats would be joining the prime minister to opine about the untrustworthiness of journalists!

Released on bail, my son got home at eleven the next morning. Then I learned that during the night he was on the verge of being released from jail when he phoned a minister and asked to stay the night. He didn't want the police's sympathy. In accordance with the law, he posted bail in court before coming home.

By dawn, everything had boiled over. The state electrical engineers union and the electrical workers union didn't just announce a strike, they had started striking. It wasn't just about the dead donkey or my son's arrest; it was about the generalists' conspiracy against the specialists, the disrespect they had shown and their having gone too far. By spending one night in jail, my son had become a martyr, a hero, an important political leader and the lynchpin uniting an entire arm of the economy. By noon, doctors went on strike. An hour later, the transportation union. Don't ask what bus drivers and bus cleaners have to do with electrical engineers. Lawyers don't have anything to do with engineers either, but when the Forestry Department workers went on strike with everyone else, the lawyers followed suit. Not to mention that university instructors had been among the first to strike. By evening, the news was that street cleaners would go on strike, as well as all of the state's pharmacists. Everything shut down. The dairy men come from the surrounding villages to sell their milk stopped that night; they were scared that students would accost them in the street to rob them and steal their bicycles. Rickshaw drivers barricaded themselves at home so that hoodlums couldn't stop them and demand being ferried around town all night for free. The rumor spread that there was a plane at the airport with a bomb on board, but it proved to be false. Truth be told, across the state, for two or three days, it felt like a wolf was on the loose.

Thirteen

So, the story of the donkey has ended.

But there are a couple of things I had meant to say that I want to get to now. After this thoroughgoing statewide shake-up, our son became the head of his union and the leader of the All-India Electrical Engineers Union. In accordance with his increased power, his dislike for the generalists grew even more.

However, thoroughgoing statewide shake-up or not, ordinary bureaucrats weren't really affected. They let the electrical engineers union and the chief minister turn the matter into an internal political affair, and they, the ordinary bureaucrats, stood to the side as the two groups fought. They watched, as would normal spectators, friends, advice-givers and sounding boards for the combatants. When an agreement was finally reached, it was between the electricity minister and the electrical engineers union, and ordinary bureaucrats were permitted to voice support for both sides: they praised my son's intellectual fury and his emotional intelligence, as well as the electricity ministry's sensible patience; and how, despite the furious activity, my son had kept his cool in an atmosphere of gross insults. So, in the agreement that was struck between the two groups, the work of the ordinary bureaucrats was nothing more than asking questions of both sides in preparation for the agreement, and then getting both sides to sign it.

The person who faired the best throughout this mess was our donkey son. Now people felt a great love for him. He could derail the system with one flick of his hand! High-ranking officials trembled when they heard his name. People on the street rifled through the day's paper to read what he had last said. In Delhi, ten members of parliament banded together to invite him to join the Rajya Sabha, and he was called on by his party's high command to take a seat there. But our son decided to stay and work in Lucknow because there he could earn his full salary without actually working. It turned out that the politician running the Subhash Nagar–Sonia Vihar scheme was a sub-sub-deputy of one of the ten parliament members who had asked him to come to Delhi. And now that politician considered my son a godfather.

Fourteen

Our washerman's opinion was different. He said that even though our son shot a donkey, all the donkeys of the city forgave him.

'You see, your son has called for a strike six times in six months. And they've been long strikes. Terylene and terrycloth have ruined us washermen, it's cut into our ironing piecework. It's just like barbers. Now people wear their hair long. There's not the need for barbers. And yet people are dying their hair more. That's what barbers are living by. It's the same as our ironing. Whenever your son calls for an electricity strike, then all home laundries are useless. Their electric irons don't work.'

'So, then what happens?'

'That's when your clothes start piling up at our place. We load up our donkeys like in the days gone by and go to the washing ghats. Then we bring them back and iron them with our coal irons. Our donkey feels better when our business is thriving, and it's thanks to your son. Our donkeys know that they owe everything to your son.'

In short, no matter how luxurious is the lion's pelt that our son might wear, in our washerman's eyes, he's the king of the donkeys.

Fifteen

My son turned down the opportunity to become a member of the Rajya Sabha because he thought that a job with four free assistants, a free car, free trips and no salary was beneath him. Then he was called to a dinner with the state's chief secretary. There, in an effort to build up his image, instead of drinking whiskey, he drank only pineapple juice. When he came home, he said to my wife, 'Mummyji, see, I'm not your donkey anymore.'

Will these ten members of parliament—who are so on edge that even when alone they look around with great concern, then jump when they see their shadows—invite my son to come join them, even though they are acting on their own initiative? And will they suddenly have the gall to make suggestions to the party's high command in public? Who is behind this?

I spoke on the subject: 'Son, you're right. Now you're no longer your Mummy's donkey. But who is behind these ten members of parliament who are kicking you to join politics? Don't forget that you don't know who it is and, without knowing, you can be made into someone else's donkey. Try to find out for yourself who wants to make you their donkey, and who's going to be your papa and mummy now.'

17

What Went Wrong with Family Planning?

The data from the 1991 Indian census has been released. Over the past ten years, the population of the country has risen at a clip of just above 23 per cent, for a total of 843,430,000 people. In the same period, just in Uttar Pradesh, there was a 25.4 per cent increase; the population there is 140,000,000, or one out of six of India's people lives in this starving state. Orissa, another starving state, has a population of 31,600,000. Its increase was around 20 per cent. So, on the one hand, you have approval of the World Bank for the country's sound family planning strategy, and, on the other hand, you see the census data. This data shows a terrifying explosion in the population, and it tears to shreds any claims of the success of family planning.

HEALTH AND FAMILY WELFARE MINISTRY

(On the verandahs, in the alleys and in the rooms, there's an atmosphere of mourning and apprehensive silence. In a conference room, people are talking quietly as they busily put into place the last details of a meeting.

The meeting is called in a hurry. There are fifteen people in the air-conditioned room. Contrary to expectations, they look happy. Looking at them, you would think they are successful people; this is what they want you to see. Only the Minister's expression seems a little slack, but this might just be a birth defect.

(The meeting begins. Glasses of water, coffee and biscuits.)

MINISTER: How did this happen? The statistics from every monthly report showed the great success of the family-planning initiative. The birth rate was lowering. So, suddenly why this explosion in population?

ONE WILY MEMBER: The population statistics are entirely fabricated. They've been made up to make us look bad.

MINISTER: It's possible, but this excuse is a little too convenient. People won't believe it. What about another reason?

(His questioning glance passes over the face of each and every member until it comes to rest upon the Press Secretary's. According to protocol, the Press Secretary stands up and starts speaking self-righteously and with great confidence.)

PRESS SECRETARY: Everyone knows that our information campaign was one hundred per cent effective. Now who can claim not to know the names of the Masti, Nirodh and Kamasutra brand condoms? Our jingle is more popular than the national anthem. You too must have memorized the Malady birth-control pill jingle, 'Ma-lady, O, ma-lady, it will give you so much pleasure, ma-lady.' Now kids everywhere know this tune.

MINISTER: It was adults who should have known it.

PRESS SECRETARY: Please be patient, sir. In ten or so years, these kids will be adults.

ANOTHER MEMBER: By then, the population will be two and a half billion!

PRESS SECRETARY: Why are you worrying? By then, you'll be retired.

THIRD MEMBER: Because we're talking about spreading information, I have to say that the two ads for condoms are nonsense. The Kamasutra one is indecent.

PRESS SECRETARY: Please forgive me, but can you talk about the business of having kids, or not having kids, in some way that isn't indecent? I want to have an ad that shows that all creation comes out of indecency just like a lotus grows in mud.

THIRD MEMBER: Stop, stop! You didn't hear me through. The second ad, for Masti condoms, it's just plain wrong. There's a galloping horse . . .

MINISTER (gravely): Is the condom for horses?

PRESS SECRETARY: It's not about condoms or horses, sir, it's about spreading information. Our survey says that little kids sit in front of a TV for hours on end just to see soft-serve ice cream and horses.

MINISTER: So, it's all for kids? Did you do anything at all for adults?

PRESS SECRETARY: Of course, sir! For women, we have Lady's Friend, and for men, we have Masti condoms.

ONE MEMBER (whispering into ANOTHER MEMBER'S ear): Too bad that he doesn't give men a lady friend and women some foreplay.

(The SECOND MAN smiles from ear to ear, as though he was about to receive a prize for being a man.)

MINISTER: We've talked a lot about the public information campaign, so let's move on to implementation. How did things go so wrong?

ONE MEMBER: But I thought the whole initiative was public information?

(The MINISTER stares at him. Then a FOURTH MEMBER speaks.)

FOURTH MEMBER: In all honesty, nothing went wrong. The birthrate declined as much as we could have hoped for. But the death rate made up for it by being horrible. What happened was that people forgot to die. The infant mortality rate is practically zero.

MINISTER: Where's the proof?

FOURTH MEMBER: It's in the statistics. But you can see for yourself. Going by in the car, you must have seen it. Everyone in the street has kids—living kids. Not even one child walking down the street is dead.

(The MINISTER stops to think about this . . . silence . . . then he speaks.)

MINISTER: Any suggestions for the death rate?

FOURTH MEMBER: We can ask for something from the Labor Ministry. Like the Golden Handshake scheme. Give a lump sum payment to non-essential workers and government officers and have them retire early. Why can't we give some incentive to our old people and senior citizens so they will want to speed along to heaven? Give them attractive compensation and explain to them that it's not possible to continue living for as long as they want. For population control, birth and death rates have to be in harmony.

MINISTER: I see. Your suggestion is that our strategy should focus on increasing the death rate, along with lowering the birth rate. We'll have to consider this.

ONE MEMBER: We'll have to ask the World Bank as well.

18

Curfew in the City

As soon as unrest was on the horizon, the district magistrate imposed a curfew on the city. But no mention of curfews can be found in any criminal law book, just as no mention of public bathrooms can be found in any health manual. A curfew isn't a word; it's a thing. In fact, it becomes possible due to an injunction hidden within the Indian Penal Code, Section 144. But, in any case, when you pass by a public bathroom you have to plug your nose, and when a curfew goes into effect, people (especially the poor) have to suffer through all sorts of torments. It's a form of terror. Even dogs and cats know that.

Curfews are a part of a savage medieval world full of barbarity, and yet today's world is barbarous too. Curfews were imported to India from Britain, and imported to Britain from Europe. As soon as the alarm bell was rung announcing imminent danger, the hearth fires were quickly tamped down. This meant that wooden houses were in danger of burning down, and yet the attackers passed by without entering the houses since they couldn't see any light inside. This was a common event in medieval Europe. The only people allowed to keep their fires going were the barbers of Venice. Like medieval Indian barbers, they were also surgeons; in an emergency, their service might be needed. In Britain, the customs of ringing the alarm started in the time of Alfred the Great and was made common by William the Conqueror. Every night, the curfew bell was sounded. This practice fell away for a time, but was later revived. In 1848, alarm bells were sounded in Sussex, Hastings and other areas. In 1918, during World War I, the British Board of Trade used sirens to direct people to save their coal or to turn off their lights. This practice eventually stopped. But military leaders understood the utility of this practice. In 1920, it was practised in Ireland. In 1950, in Cyprus. And Germany used it in the lands it occupied during World War II.

Now, in India, we've stopped using sirens, but we've held onto curfews like they're a foolproof remedy against insurrection. In an emergency, the powers that be in India can't think of anything else to do but put in place a curfew, pretend everything is good and go on their merry way.

Under the curfew, city residents suffer in ever yet new ways. Sometimes the local edition of the *Times of India* runs a column called 'Triveni Talk', dedicated to news from Prayagraj, that is, Allahabad. It's not about Akshayavat or Bhardwaj. It's basically an Allahabadi police blotter.

Several days ago, they published a curfew story. In Nakhas Kohna, a woman left her home, and some Central Reserve Police Force (CRPF) soldiers immediately seized her. They carried her off into a building at a local college. Police officers were nearby. The neighborhood people stayed back, but they called out to the officers. Hearing their shouts, the police forbade them to advance. Maybe they thought that the CRPF soldiers were enrolling the woman as a non-traditional student at school. But then a police officer, short in stature, stepped up. He saved the woman and severely punished the CRPF soldiers, meaning, he removed them from curfew duty and sent them back to the barracks.

Four years ago, Vibhuti Narain Rai published a novel *Curfew in the City*. It was the same type of story, only more tragic. Based upon the neighborhood names, it was clear the novel was about Allahabad and nowhere else. The novel included some truly terrifying incidents.

The incident with the girl went like this.

The girl was still at school when the curfew went into effect. She left school in a hurry and was racing home when she was abducted in an alley: two strong hands suddenly grabbed her from behind a half-closed gate and thrust her into a shop. And yet, people were around. People in the neighborhood watched in silence from behind windows and cracked-open doors. But they didn't say anything.

Even though the author of *Curfew in the City* is a high-ranking police officer, it read like a police melodrama. So, what was the gist of the story? The curfew was put in place to avoid mayhem, but if the curfew hadn't been in place, then the girl wouldn't have been raped in an alley . . . I had dismissed this scene as fiction, but then, in Allahabad during the last curfew, the CRPF soldiers proved I was wrong. Is this an instance of life copying art?

The *Times of India* columnist wrote, 'The Allahabad Police doesn't treat everyone as equal under the law. They treat soldiers as though they're better than common citizens.' Perhaps our respected columnist doesn't know what Churchill said. During World War II, Allied armies complained about British soldiers acting superior. Churchill responded, 'Why be apologetic about Anglo–Saxon superiority? We are superior!'

19

A Country of 820 Million Peoples

He was building a building in a big, open field next to his neighborhood. It was surrounded by high walls, and it had an enormous gate. There were barracks inside, as well as some large buildings. I addressed my old schoolmate, 'What kind of building is this?'

'It's the community's assembly hall.'

'To me it looks just like a jail,' I said.

'Me, too,' he answered. 'Actually, this building is a jail. Over there, on the corner, that building's the assembly hall. Everything else is a jail.'

Villagers called him Gajodhar. His real name was Gadadhar Prasad, BA. He was his community's main political leader. He believed in carrying out the Mandal Commission's recommendations, but he wasn't personally interested in the details. He wasn't interested in work quotas.

He started to explain, 'The All India Muslim Personal Law Board is our model. You Brahmins should learn from them too.'

He went on, 'They just met in Jaipur, right? They decided to build their own Islamic courts for Muslim families. It's a great idea. We should do it too—every community should. They say that the high courts and the Supreme Court take too long to hand down their verdicts, and it costs too much money, and sometimes the verdicts run counter to their religious beliefs. And they're right. They are also making mobile courts. They can travel from village to village, rendering verdicts for Muslim women. They can do it right on their doorsteps, and without court fees.'

'Those poor Muslim women need TB pills more than they need the law,' I said. 'Why can't they have mobile pharmacies?'

'That's for the government to do,' he said. 'Our community has always had panchayats. People who break from the community face judgment there. We mete punishment. Sometimes, we excommunicate them, or we impose a fine that goes back to the community. Now we're thinking about making our own courts, like the Muslim Board. We can piss as far as them, right!'

'What does that have to do with the law?' I asked, startled at the coarseness of what my friend had just said.

'I mean, we're not inferior to them,' he explained. 'If they're building their own courts to replace the government ones, why can't we?'

'And then all the other communities . . .'

'They can too! Why not?'

'But, my friend,' I said, 'You're building a jail, not a court.'

'Because, unlike Muslims, we're not doing this only half way,' he said. 'If you have a court, you need a jail too. You have to even have a gallows. Several years ago in Mathura, one community's panchayat condemned a young man to death. The poor soul had to be hung from a tree. Right now, in Muzaffarabad, some boy ran off with some girl and came back married. Their community wanted to hang them. So, what were they forced to do? Slit their throats right then and there. We want to do everything right. If we have a court, we'll have a jail, and we'll have a gallows.'

'And the police?'

'The police aren't going anywhere. If they did, who would represent the accused?' Suddenly, he got all worked up, 'Pandit, we're even going to build our own Vidhan Sabha. Sometimes, the national law ignores our traditions and customs. It . . . our . . . it . . . how should I put it? It wounds us, our identity. With our own legislature, our identity will be preserved.'

He went on, 'Like you, Pandit, you Brahmins. Your identity should be preserved, right? You don't want to touch me, you don't want to drink water that I've touched. So don't touch me, don't drink the water. And I'll not touch you, I won't drink your water. What sort of law is it that says you're forced to drink the water I serve you? This prohibition against touching, or the tradition of sati or your caste marriage rules, they're all *your* identity. Pandit, preserve them! Like the Muslim Personal Law Board, you carry on with your own laws, and you make your own courts!'

'But what about the country's constitution?'

'So what about it? With free courts, the Muslim Law Board will get around the constitution, and everyone else can too.'

'But then we'll return to just being hundreds of tribes. What about our national identity? What will happen to our country?'

'Nothing will happen to it! If there's 820 million people in India, then we'll become a country of 820 million peoples. "Unity in diversity and diversity in unity . . ."— that's the government catch phrase. Tell me, as far as "unity in diversity" goes, what possibly will the government be able to come up with to compete with our scheme?'

20

Tiger Hunting

Since my youth, I've been fond of hunting. I didn't know it then; it was only when Wilson told me that I realized it. That was in Nainital. I happened to meet Wilson there. He was a respected member of the Forestry Department. Afterward, since I was also a respected member of the Forestry Department, we became close friends.

One day, I learned that Wilson was fond of hunting. That day, he learned that I was too. From there, everything followed quite naturally.

Usually, Wilson would wear clean, pressed clothes and an expensive suit. He would wear bright American ties with scenes from nature or with images of film stars. One day, I saw him wearing a dirty khaki coat and a pair of old breeches cinched to his waist with the help of a leather belt. He was wearing big, thick shoes, and he hadn't shaved in four or five days. He was wearing an old hat tied under his chin with a strap, and he was walking with his legs spread. His eyes were bloodshot, and his breath smelled of cheap liquor. A rifle was slung over his shoulder. It looked like a long club.

I was shocked to see him in this state.

'Hey, you look just like a dyed-in-the-wool hunter. Where are you coming from?'

'Hunter? You didn't know? I've bagged fifty-something tigers. I've been hunting, and I'm going back right now. Why don't you come with me?'

At four o'clock that afternoon, we arrived in the jungle with our rifles in tow. I knew this location. We were there to hunt tigers, but that part of the jungle was especially well known as a good place for taking a stroll due to the absence of tigers.

Suddenly, the bushes shook roughly, and a terrifying animal leaped out. Worried for his life, Wilson pointed the butt of his rifle in its direction. The animal took a leap in the opposite direction and disappeared.

I watched him as he pointed the butt of the rifle into the bushes.

Wilson said, 'Sometimes showing the butt of the rifle instead of its barrel has a psychological effect on tigers. They think the butt is a huge barrel, and they get scared. That's why I pointed the butt.'

I didn't interrupt him, and so he stopped on his own. Then he said, 'One way or another, that was a tiger cub, for sure.'

'No, Wilson,' I said, sure of myself. 'That wasn't a tiger cub. It was a rabbit. I've bagged about fifty rabbits. The first one was in the Vindhya Range when I was fifteen or so.'

As though recalling something, Wilson repeated the English word, 'Rabbit?' Then he explained, 'You mean what we call chaugada or khargosh? You can find those all over northern India!'

'Just like you can find different types of bears—black bears, white bears—it's the same with rabbits. You have black ones, white ones, even brown ones.'

He put his hand on my shoulder and said, 'So, admit it, partner. You're an experienced hunter, as well. You've been hunting since you were fifteen!'

That day, I looked back over my past and realized that just like some people are born fools, and some are born poets, I was born a hunter.

The next day, we set out for a different jungle because the first day's tigerless jungle seemed no longer entirely tiger-free.

Dear readers, for you to appreciate this story, first I have to tell you about the geographical features of this area. To the north and south, there were flat-topped mountains rising 700 feet above sea level. From the left of the south to the right of the north, that is, in the east, there were more 700-feet-tall mountains. And from the left of the north and the right of the south, meaning, in the west, there were more 700-feet-tall mountains. And in the middle? More of the same 700-feet-tall mountains that could be found to the north, south, east and west. But there was no pass through these mountains, and, when you added this all up, it was a truly terrifying region. The jungle was full of mango and date trees, as well as bamboo and acacia trees and, in between, there were the frightening, though low-lying, bushes of wild jujube, karonda and black nightshade. These bushes were so puny that a tiger couldn't sit in them;

it would have to lie down. So, a hunter had to lie down in each and every clump to find out if a tiger was hiding there. From time to time, the tiger and the hunter were aware that they were lying down next to each other, and yet the bushes were too thick for one to reach the other.

You could say that it wasn't a jungle but an ordinary orchard. But there's a big difference between a jungle and an orchard. An orchard is planted according to a plan. Because there was no rhyme or reason to the way the trees were arranged there, I thought of it then, and now, and will so too in the future, as pure jungle.

That day, we were wearing rubber-soled boots. We walked in silence. We searched the entire area, but we didn't see neither hide nor hair of any tiger. The problem was that our rubber-soled boots had been so quiet that the tigers remained sleeping in the bushes. Once we made it to the far edge of the trees, we realized our mistake. When we left the jungle that day, we decided to wear leather shoes the next day so that the tigers would hear us coming and spring to life.

The next day, a local hunter said that a dead cow had been found in the area. A tiger had killed it, and he was waiting for the tiger to return.

When we set off that day, our hearts were beating wildly. Waves of anticipation swept over us. Wilson's face was ashen; he hadn't slept a wink all night. I was sweating bullets. This was not because I was afraid; no, it was out of happiness that my blood pressure was rising! Our hands were shaking because we were filled with glee, and our feet were wobbling because we were trying to walk fast!

We took a different road so that we would be late. That is, we delayed our arrival until after the tiger should have returned to the 'kill'. Here, it's necessary for me to say that while some hunters wait at the kill site for the tiger to return, in fact, tigers and poets don't work on a time schedule. You can get to the kill site ahead of schedule, but you'll still be sorely disappointed when the tiger doesn't show up. So why not save yourself from wasting your time and wait until the tiger gets there first? I'm speaking from experience.

Well, back to the story.

So, that day, we took a different road to get to the kill site. The road map in my hand had red marks to indicate the places where a tiger had killed cows, and a blue mark to show where a tiger had killed a person. And yet, since no such occasion had come to pass, there was no red, and no blue, on the map. It was completely unmarked, except for the legend's red and blue explanatory marks.

The map had two black lines, one to indicate the cement road and one for the railway line that went through the area. There was a symbol to mark a roadside park as well. But we didn't especially trust the map due to how when using it to find our way out of town, we were just pushed back further into town. But we were hunters, and so we had to have a map, and we had to use it.

As we neared the trees, we first had to pass through a swamp. We got held up there by four small footprints. The local hunter said that they were goat prints, but Wilson stubbornly insisted they were tiger tracks. He got out a tape measure, measured the prints and told us all about the tiger. From the measurements, he could tell that it was a male, not a female; it was fifteen years old, its front left leg was wounded on its knee and its right leg was lame. It was ten feet, eleven and a half inches long. It was brown. It was ferocious. It was deadly . . . so on and so forth.

Then, sparrows started singing. Wilson said that the tiger had been there just five minutes earlier because sparrows start singing exactly five minutes after a tiger leaves an area.

We stepped forward, and then, without any warning, Wilson dove to the ground and looked sideways into the bushes. I caught on that an animal was hunkering to the ground nearby.

Sparrows were still circling overhead. I grabbed one and put it in my pocket to remind myself that the tiger had left the area five minutes earlier.

At this point, the kill site was still almost 200 metres away. I scanned the scene as I advanced. Then, a bush shook violently, and, before I could gain control of my rifle, a tiger was standing right in front of me.

Dear readers, please think of the situation I was in. There was no one to help me, and a tiger was growling ferociously right in front of me. But I didn't lose courage. I released the safety, I pointed the gun at the tiger and I pulled the trigger. Nothing happened. The cartridge was caught in the magazine.

Perhaps the tiger had been scared before. But seeing my gun malfunction, it smiled with pure happiness. It leaped onto me. The rifle slipped from my hands and fell far away.

The tiger thought that one swipe of his paw would fell me. It didn't. We started wrestling. The tiger lived up to its name. I did too. But for how long could I keep it up? In reality, I tired quickly, and the tiger brought me to the ground. It stood over my prostrate body. It killed me. It ate me up.

You will say that I've exaggerated the story, and that's true. The truth of the matter is that the tiger didn't kill me, and it didn't eat me up. When it raised its paw to strike the death blow, I screamed, 'Tiger Uncle, don't kill me!'

'How could I kill you when you've become like a nephew to me?' the tiger roared. Then he asked, 'But, tell me, why do you want to live?'

'Tiger Uncle,' I said, 'what other hunter has ever stared you in the mouth? Hunters brag of confronting you. But I have wrestled you. I have stared into your roaring mouth. You don't know me. I'm a servant of literature and will remain so until my dying day. Yet, where I'm from, we suffer from a lack of hunting stories. If I live, I want to write this up as a story. Then, Tiger Uncle, I'll return and lie down here just like I am now.'

'I'm a tiger, you're a brave man. Go write your stories,' the tiger said.

Five minutes later, the sparrow started chirping again in my pocket. I woke up. I was lying on the ground eight metres from Wilson. I remember my encounter with the tiger only with considerable effort.

Dear readers, it could be said that there's some exaggeration in this account, but, in the end, who wants a hunting story without a little exaggeration?

21

First Letter to My Honorable Friend
(On Foreign Travels)

Lucknow
26 September 1965

My friend,

Your letter is in front of me. The return address is Graceland Avenue, Indianapolis, Indiana. And my address is there: Lucknow, Uttar Pradesh, India. Did you write out my address not to make sure the letter reached me, but only to embarrass me?

It was bound to happen. I never managed to get invited by some institute over there, and I never bothered to inveigle my way into a delegation from here bound for there. I've never entered the private sector; the public sector has never let me go. When I heard that there was a problem with foreign aid, I didn't think the news was made up, I accepted it for fact. And then it became fact. And you left for there, and I stayed here and, with a little geographical displacement, our friendship was riven asunder.

Until recently, we were equals. When the British granted us Independence and left, we took their lifestyle to be the ideal, even though we considered it degrading to mimic their moral bearing. We were both educated (meaning, we spoke English). We had cars (not homemade jalopies—real *foreign* cars). Our children went to convent schools (where their school mistresses spoke to them in Hinglish—tumhara Mummy tumko agar book nahin denga to tumko punish milenga). We earned good money. All sorts of bureaucrats and businessmen were our friends. We were obsessed with avoiding income tax. We were white-collar workers. We were real, and whoever the 'people' were, they were like forged documents, torn up and tossed into the trash can. Now, I'm the same person, but as soon as you got to America, you changed. There, your status changed, and, since in this chaos I was unable to go to America, you brutally tossed me aside.

But don't think I'm jealous. I'm only repeating the mantras of modern sociology. Actually, I'm happy you got to go to America. As soon as you get back, even before you say 'apartment' instead of 'flat', 'long-distance call' instead of 'trunk call', before all of that, I'll jump for joy and say, 'Oh my gosh, it's my friend! He's back from America!' God's honest truth.

Outside of India, there are many countries. You must surely know that among them there is Pakistan, Sri Lanka and Nepal. On Earth, there is also Algeria, Ghana and Nigeria. Argentina is there too, and Brazil. These are perhaps on the same level as us, as far as misfortunes go. But your attitude is the best. When we leave India, is it to see others' misfortune, or forget ours? If it's to see misfortune, don't we have enough here? So, for Indian tourists, there are only two places to go: Europe or North America. We have too many travel narratives about Europe and the United States. A little while ago, our travel narratives were set in the dust of Tibet, and the books sported colorful covers. They were amazing. But those foreigners looking for risky adventures in far-flung forests, mountains, mighty oceans or at the ends of the earth are novices. So, the fact that you followed the lead of experienced Indians speaks well for you. You set off on the path of great beings—you travelled the very route suggested by the ads of Pan American Airways!

The way you spoke of America in your letter pleased me even more. You wrote about what those who know America (especially travel writers) write about to their friends. You wrote about American women, who are found either in bathing suits on beaches, or driving fast cars. You also applied the thinking of Karl Jaspers and Nietzsche to New York's Theater District, the Arizonan desert, Greenwich Village, Beatniks and the idle youth of both sexes. There's a lot of money there and even more cars. Also, drinking liquor is easy. You researched these topics with great skill and provided great detail. But, just as all of our travel writers do, you remain silent in front of American social and political foibles and scientific and technological blind spots. And though before going to America you were as far from being a writer as you were geographically from America, now, just like all Indian writers who came before you, you're thinking of publishing in Indian weeklies your *Memoirs of My American Travels*.

I've read so many things in this genre that I know what you will write—at which historical location, with which girl, at which time you came around to saying what and how, and due to what circumstances she suddenly stopped laughing and started listening. These stories show the clear traces of influence from Sarat Chandra's melodramatic novels; they're classic Eastern fare. You'll say everything, but you won't have the courage to say at which historical location what history actually took place. So, this will be your *Memoirs of My American Travels*. In this way, you'll join those writers who return from Europe and America and give birth to immortal stories and ravishing adventures for our eternally countrified Indian minds. So you will lend support to the idea that, for India, the struggles of Africa's blacks aren't important, the only important thing is white girls lounging on Miami Beach.

You've written that you are about to send the first installment of your travelogue to a weekly. You've asked for advice. By way of advice, I'm sending you one of my travelogues, which you can use as an example. Where was your old house before you built a bungalow on the outskirts of the city? In Marwari Alley, right? I took a trip there. I'm including a section of the narrative below.

'. . . on the street, there were some three-wheeled vehicles, which we call rickshaws. They were being driven by dirty, skinny animals, that is, one type of men. Some white-collar workers were seated in the back, another type of men. There was an enormous rickshaw traffic jam. My spirits were sinking. Then, Marwari

Alley appeared, and we turned into it. I was surprised to find myself still alive after all the rickshaws, cars and horse-drawn carts—and just narrowly escaping getting crushed by several huge trucks.

'My friend's house was 150 feet down the alley. The alley was about seven feet wide. I had just left the rickshaw when an animal grabbed my foot. I looked down and saw that it had my sandal in its hand. Looking very carefully, I saw that it was an eleven-year-old boy. He was blathering something. Before I could say anything, he set to cleaning my sandals. He had sores all around his mouth, and I couldn't make out what he was saying. It was clear that he wasn't pleading to be placed in a children's home or to argue on behalf of compulsory education. While he was polishing to my sandals, I took a good look at the alley.

'On both sides, there were open sewers. Sewage water was draining noisily from a couple of broken pipes. When the water hit the ground, it sprang up in delightful spray, like a mini Niagara Falls. Three stark naked boys were sitting by the open sewer taking advantage of the dirty freedoms of youth.

'The falling water was also splattering a man. He didn't have hands or legs. He was seated on the ground. He kept saying *heh-heh*, and with each *heh*, he slid an inch further along. At the same time, he pushed along a tin bowl, in which there were several coins. People gave him a wide berth, like they did the sewers, or they stepped over him. Ahead, there was a sweet seller's shop with sixteen square feet chock-full of sweets. Flies were protecting the sweets, and the philosophy of non-violence was protecting the flies. Right then, the sweet seller was vehemently cursing the disabled man for being there.

'Nearby, there was that sort of thing that you might find anywhere, I mean, a paan stall. Paan spittle decorated the alleyway in a span from one open sewer to the other. There was a poster on the wall. The wall was new. It was made of cement and looked strong; it looked like the builder had built it for himself, not for the government. The poster was ripped and torn, but still you could make out the words, *VOTE FOR BABU BANSGOPAL*.

'Mostly moneylenders and old money lived in the alley.

'I retrieved my sandals, and, somehow, I advanced up to the sweet shop. There, I made plans to progress further. My friend's house was still 120 feet away . . .'

My friend, this is the travelogue of trying to get to your old house. You can use it as an example. I look forward to seeing how my dear friend, whose old house was in Marwari Alley, will slip in our dreams of heaven into your descriptions of America.

Yours,
Shrilal Shukla

22

Second Letter to My Honorable Friend (About Your 'Men')

Lucknow
26 September 1965

My friend,
I take it from your letter that your business in Delhi has reached a standstill. You wrote that your 'men' at the office in question had become some other people's 'men'.

Before I give you some advice, I want to take a minute to talk about this 'rule of men' business.

What's democracy? In India, even little kids know that it's the rule of the people, for the people, by the people. As for 'my men', we have our great cultural traditions to thank. History bears witness to . . .

Well, actually, let's not go there. I'll get too riled up.

In India, nothing gets done without 'my man'. This is true about each and every thing. A leaf doesn't move without 'my man', and so for any business, well, it's a much bigger deal because income tax officers are involved. I'll tell you a story, it's rather ordinary, but, anyway, it's about sales tax.

Not so long ago, it happened that I had to buy shoes. Now, don't think that I was a fool and went to the market. If I had done that, then I would have spent a lot of money for something that may have looked like a pair of shoes when it wasn't necessarily a pair of shoes.

My problem was different. I thought about how there are two well-known ways of buying shoes, and I'd have to choose one. Either spend twenty-five years acquiring the necessary expert knowledge to become a cobbler myself, or ready my 'men' and buy shoes with their help.

Obviously, I chose the latter. I called one of my 'men'. He was a former member of the legislature with the specialization that the moment required. He called the former secretary of the shoe-sellers union (an unpaid position). The former secretary phoned me. 'Don't worry,' he said. 'I know the Bright Shoe people. We can go tonight. You'll get some great shoes.' Then he added, in the way of the promises bandied about in romantic films, 'Don't worry. Everything will work out in the end.'

I wanted to have one more 'man' with me. I asked in a whisper, 'I've a friend who lives in Pata Nala. He knows all about shoes. He's always talking about them. He knows a good pair from bad. Can I bring him too?'

He agreed.

He was a well-known journalist, but then he couldn't make it. He had gone to the train station. It turned out that one of his 'men' had to go to Delhi on the overnight train, but he couldn't get a reservation. The journalist had a 'man' in the booking office, who had a 'man' in the reservation office, who . . .

The three of us arrived at the store. But the 'man' of the former secretary of the shoe-sellers union wasn't there. We learned that he had a 'man' who had to buy some saris, so he had taken him to a sari shop owned by one of his other 'men'. The accountant was running the shop for the moment. He was talking to a lawyer. The accountant greeted us very politely, 'Just a minute, please. If you don't mind, he was here first, and he's in a hurry.'

We listened to their conversation. A new aspect of the 'rule of men' became clear. I had known that in order to get anything done, you had to have a 'man' absolutely everywhere, but now . . .

The problem was that the water metre at the shopkeeper's house had broken a while ago. He had got one of his 'men' to fix it. But the shopkeeper was not sure how much the city was charging him each month. Try though he might, he hadn't yet been able to get the city to give him his bill. He was ready to pay, but they weren't ready to take his money.

'I'm getting the lawyer to file a case against the city,' the accountant said. 'Those people are purposely avoiding us. They want to wait so that several years down the road they will give a big bill saying we owe thousands.'

Then he put some real fire behind his words, 'But I'm not going to allow that! Nothing's going to stop me from paying on time!'

'I had a "man" in the water tax section,' my 'man' said. 'His name's Babu Ram, and he's . . .'

'Don't mention that bastard's name, Secretary, sir!' the accountant said. 'He's the "man" of the Sunshine Shoe people. He's the one behind all this crap.'

'So, go ahead with the case,' my friend said.

'That goes without saying,' the accountant said. 'But, right now, the judge is the chairman's "man". He's being transferred. The person coming in his place is one of my uncle's "men". So, I'm waiting.'

My friend, over the course of the next half hour, I managed to buy a pair of shoes. My 'men' praised my purchase, saying how their help had saved me from paying sales tax and from the exorbitant prices of other shoe stores.

But don't ask what happened to that pair of shoes. It's enough to say that after wearing them for ten days, I stuck them in a corner where their life as a pair of shoes came to an end and they took up their place as a traditional Indian weapon of peace and war. But that's another story.

So, consider the situation. Even though I had my 'men', I had to go through this whole rigmarole for just a small purchase. So, if I didn't have a 'man', and if the stakes of the business interaction were much greater, then what? So, I'm saying, don't go ahead with your business in Delhi.

My friend, my 'men'! Please repeat these two words ten times, and then lick your lips once, twice, three times. Feel the music, feel the deadly weight, of these words and tomorrow, in the early morning, please return to your city and open a shop here.

Yours,
Shrilal Shukla

23

Third Letter to My Honorable Friend (About Memorial Services)

Lucknow
27 February 1966

My friend,

Just yesterday, I read in a monthly magazine an article full of pictures and poetry about a memorial service held in your city. I was happy to learn that you were the person in charge of the memorial for the deceased prime minister, and that Babu Ramadhar was kept on the sidelines. In your speech, the comparisons you used to describe the deceased politician, though old-fashioned, were quite apt, especially the ones about the sun and fog. Some of the poetry sung at the memorial was really wonderful. One was just like the poetry I heard on All India Radio a couple of days ago during the eulogies sung at a poetry event where one poet was even better than playback singer Mohammad Rafi.

You have attended around 150 such memorials, and whenever Babu Ramadhar isn't available to be the master of ceremonies, the duty has fallen on you. I understand your grief. These days in my town, I had to go to a memorial service. I'll give you the report. After reading it, tell me whether you can understand my sadness.

Last year, you bought a Karuna Shankar Dafedar painting. He's no longer with us. The very days when you were busy with the prime minister's memorial service, Dafedar was killed in a car accident here. We intellectuals were very sad, and we agreed to hold a memorial service to acknowledge this great artist's passing.

It was early afternoon. We met in a park across from a coffee shop in a park that had a bad reputation. Usually, people went there to kiss and make out, or to pee. One friend objected to holding the memorial service there, but I explained to him that if the emotion behind it was true, then it didn't matter where the service took place. Anyway, if you look around, you see that young men and women use libraries for dating venues, offices are used as coffee shops and coffee shops are used for . . .

Our big group was comprised of painters, writers, journalists and some university professors. For variety, there were also two bureaucrats, three politicians, one shopkeeper (the coffee shop manager) and two manual laborers (two waiters from the shop). The autumn's warm afternoon sun fell on pretty English flowers whose names, should we go through them all here, would be its own story, as they are untranslatable into any Indian language. The memorial service began. We sat down on a rug with heavy hearts and heavy stomachs.

'Brothers and sisters . . .' the master of ceremonies began.

('Sisters' was an exaggeration: there was only one woman there.)

'Brothers and sisters, we are gathered here today in the shadow of great sadness. Our beloved leader, the prime minister . . .'

The rumor was our master of ceremonies had invented a seed drill for farmers. He sold the newest farm implements to farmers through government agents. But this job was just an excuse because he was really an MSc. But that was just an excuse, as well, because he was a member of the National Gallery of Art and the chairman of their purchasing committee. All in all, his was a multipronged project balanced on his rather small two feet. When he was doing business, he wore a homespun kurta–pajama. At the State Legislative Council, he wore a terylene suit. For this occasion, he was wearing a sherwani and a garland of red roses hung from his neck.

'. . . today, the entire nation mourns his unexpected passing. He was the great leader of our nation . . .'

I whispered into his ear, 'Karuna Shankar Dafedar has died. This is *his* memorial service, not the prime minister's.'

He nodded his head to indicate there was nothing to worry about.

Because there was nowhere to get paan in the park, everyone had already stuffed paan in their mouths, and they were slowly chewing away.

'In this time of grief, we have sustained another wound. You all know quite well our country's great artist Sir Karuna Shankar Mansabdar . . .'

I whispered the correction, 'Dafedar.'

The master of ceremonies had up until then spoken to us in a voice suitable for a memorial service. He ignored my words.

'Mansabdari was not one of our traditional artists . . .'

'Not Mansabdar, Dafedar,' I said into his ear again.

'. . . I met *Dafedar* for the first time at the National Gallery of Art's annual show. I learned then that he was a first-class artist because . . .'

'Because he had a beard . . .' I muttered to myself.

'. . . because he was holding a first-class painting,' he said.

That was the end of his eulogy. It was the next speaker's turn. Next up was the coffee shop manager. He had spent more time with Dafedar Sahib in the coffee shop than most of the men gathered there had spent with their own wives at home. But he spoke very little about Dafedar, and almost too much about new trends in painting. He spoke about painting as much as a Pandey does about pilgrimages.

The sun shone down on the flowers fluttering in the breeze. Someone right behind me lit a bidi, and its smoke started to wrap about my head. You must know that I can stand bidis only up to the time that they're not lit. I looked angrily at the smoker, and it turned out to be the only woman at the memorial service. Suddenly, I had the impression that most of the people were looking at her.

Then the third speech began.

A car had pulled up alongside the park. Someone was honking its horn incessantly. Then, I recognized who it was. The chubby man inside was an economics lecturer at the university. He had got the job from having written an article called 'The Noxious Effects of Foreign Aid in India'. He had just got back from Europe, where he had been on fellowship. For a very short time, he had been one of my best friends, and I thought that perhaps he was honking for me.

The honking disrupted the memorial service, but not too much, because the speaker was just then recounting the gory details of Dafedar's car crash in a harsh voice reminiscent of Sohrab Modi and Ramdhari Singh Dinkar. The horn-honker lost. Soon enough, my lecturer friend with his angry face came up to me, and, suddenly, he too started ogling the lone woman there.

With this, the master of ceremonies announced that my friend's speech would follow. *A professor, a thinker, a scholar . . .* ! He quickly went to sit next to the MC. Perhaps he was wondering what exactly was going on. Then he thought of something and said, 'You all know very well that literature is a mirror held up to society, but you could also say that, in one way, society is a mirror to literature . . .'

Hearing him talk out of turn about society and literature made me cringe. I figured out that he was drunk. I went to and told the MC something, but, by then, my friend was talking about something else.

The MC cut the speaker off and motioned to everyone that they should remain quiet. Playing with a sheet of paper, he continued to eulogize the new generation's great painter Sir Karuna Shankar Mansabdar's—I'm sorry—*Dafedar's*—untimely demise.

Soon, though, things returned to how they'd been before my friend's arrival. Then, stepping on the workers lying on the lawn, crunching the empty peanut shells with our shoes, spitting on the roses, putting out our hands to feel the breeze, we left the park.

But my lecturer-friend stopped in his tracks. 'It's fake! A fraud!'

'You're drunk!' the MC said angrily.

My friend had a wound on his forehead. It indicated that he had got drunk, got in a fight, and then fallen on broken glass. In the afternoon sunlight, the wound shone in a special way. Then he spoke, 'You said you'd have two minutes of silence, but you only gave 35 seconds! You've defrauded Dafedar!'

'You've gone mad!' the MC said savagely.

'Maybe. But I was looking at my watch. You defrauded him by a minute and a half!'

He turned to me to be congratulated, as though he had won a bet. The MC looked at me.

'No, it's not like that,' I said. 'It used to be that you could never put a time limit on sorrow. These days, everyone understands that 35 seconds is good enough.'

My friend, the gist is that Dafedar is no more. His paintings will have to be brought together. In a while, the National Art Gallery will want to immortalize him. It will start inquiring into his paintings.

I'm looking forward to your letter.
Yours,
Shirlal Shukla

24

The Memory of an Elephant
(From the Journal of a Promising Son)

I'm against 'mom–dad' culture, so I don't call 'dad' 'dad' but 'father'. I have a funny uncle who always says, 'You know, your dad, he's a father figure, but he's a motherfucker too!'

I don't know about that, but, in order to train me to become a future chief minister, my father had to teach me his skills. He would sometimes take me with him to work at the Uttar Pradesh Chief Minister's office. These days, under the guise of management training, he sometimes takes me to work with him at his little office at the Secretariat. I even do menial tasks for him there. People have started to believe that I've got skills too. He's the current chief minister, and I'll be the future one.

My funny uncle once said, 'It'll be just a year or two before your polishing is done.'

Those days I had to go to the college, and, in the morning, I used to ask to have my shoes polished.

I asked my uncle, 'Do you understand what polishing means?'

'I understand,' he said. 'I'm not talking about that. Your polishing will be for real. A crown will be placed on your head. In one hand, you'll have a cudgel and, in the other, a sword.'

I understood that this would be the punishment for having a revolver and AK-47 taken from my hands. A gold crown and a silver cudgel are all fine and well, but you should leave one hand free at all times to hold a revolver. I told my uncle this, adding one witticism: 'This is all the joke of democracy.'

My uncle agreed.

In any event, these days, three things are on my mind.

During the anti-corruption campaign, my father had to interrogate two of his ministers. The Irrigation Minister came in first. My father said, 'I'm hearing a lot of complaints about you. It's said that you've made off with millions in commissions in conjunction with the river initiatives.'

I was sitting silently in a corner. Management training, silent supervision—it's the same thing in different terms. It's like the risqué scenes in film magazines. You want to flee the moment you see them, but then again, once you hear the dialogue, you want to hear more.

Like my father, the Irrigation Minister was known to speak his mind. He said, 'Everyone knows I'm against corruption. Corruption must be destroyed. It's a cancer on society. To eradicate it . . .'

My father gestured for him to stop. Perhaps the Irrigation Minister recalled then that he wasn't shooting the shit on some street corner. He stopped.

'I'm theoretically a fierce opponent of corruption,' he said.

'What do you mean by theoretically?'

'Just that—theoretically. But, in practice, I don't consider it wrong to make a commission. If I don't make one, someone else will. Look here, when all of society is corrupt, why should I be the only one to push Lakshmi aside? I'm part of society. I don't want to be anti-social. But, I promise you, the very day that society wipes out corruption, I'll be the first to step forward and renounce commissions. Till then, my position will remain a theoretical opposition to corruption. That's fine, right?'

My father turned toward me, as though he was trying to teach me a lesson.

'That's fine,' he said.

The second minister, the Urban Development Minister, came in. He was a friendly looking man.

My father spoke, 'There are a lot of complaints about corruption in the Saryu Nagar Construction Initiative . . .' (Saryu Nagar isn't named after the Saryu River, but after Saryuprasad, my grandfather.) '. . . They say that not even 15 per cent of the money dedicated to the project actually gets used on the project.'

The Urban Development Minister, a creature of bad habits, laughed mockingly, 'You mean, the same amount of money that Rajiv Gandhi dedicated to the people?'

Then the minister turned serious, 'Sir, please understand one thing. This is the nature of development work. Corruption grows through development. Development happens through corruption. Please consider where the millions of rupees needed to build mansions, beautiful hotels, dazzling restaurants and bars come from, if all the money for the colony's development was spent, and spent *on time*, on streets, parks, electricity, water and Amartya Sen's old pipe-dream—I mean, schools and public-health facilities? It's the bureaucrats and middle managers who steal money from the development fund in order to build these buildings for themselves. What proof would we have of our expanding middle class, then? If it weren't for this, you'd have beautiful streets, but who would use them— the same old country bumpkins and backwater fools? All along the roads, what would there be but low-income and lower-middle-income hovels? And on the beautiful and pristine roads, what would you see, but pooping water buffalos out for a stroll? Look at long lines of expensive cars and the prosperous world lining the roads, and try to understand, sir, the infinite possibilities of corruption. Just think!'

'I'll think about it,' my father said. I, too, thought that I would think about it.

Then, the minister fell to the floor, crying uncontrollably. He had been the director general of a government department before he retired three years ago. When my father became the chief minister for the second time, his old file was immediately taken out, and a court case launched in which he was charged in a scandal involving millions of rupees. He had just been released after spending a month in jail.

It was the first time I'd ever heard my father speak so firmly. 'Stop your silly crying. Answer the questions in a straightforward fashion.'

The minister kept blubbering.

'How much money did you have to repay?'

'Twenty million,' he said, through his tears, 'Ten million to begin with, then ten million when I became director general.'

'And how much did you give?'

'Ten million. I couldn't come up with the second payment.'

'Don't lie! Our government fell the minute you became director general. The very moment I was out of office, you turned on me, you corrupt, lying son-of-a-bitch! You backstabbed me! You think I'd forget that?'

'I forget nothing. I have a good memory.'

On the wall directly behind my father's chair, there was a framed poster of an elephant, as well as pictures of birds and other animals.

My father pointed to the elephant.

'Look at this one. Do you see what it is? It's an elephant. I have the memory of an elephant!'

When the man left, I wanted to ask my father several questions. But even before I could ask, he answered them, 'He'll pay back the rest now. But he should be punished for his backstabbing too.'

No doubt.

25

Several Days in Umraonagar

1. Goats, Chickens and Ripped Shirts

There were no goats where I was seated in the bus. But, in the lap of my seatmate, there was a chicken. The goats were in the back. Back there, if a baby goat happened to be on someone's lap, or if a goat was resting on someone's knee, there were also people resting their feet beneath a goat's belly or on top of a goat's back, as they leaned against the back of the bus. In that mess, it was difficult to say where any one person's head was: it was heads upon heads upon heads.

When the bus stopped, there was no time to think about how getting off the bus required more alacrity than boarding the bus. But my chicken-friendly seatmate was more energetic than me. Like Abhimanyu, he broke through the throng of passengers, and I grabbed onto his kurta's hem. We arrived where in theory the door should have been, and, without being able to confirm this fact, we jumped down, landing face first on the ground. The briefcase that had been dangling from my hand must have got caught on someone's leg because the traveller behind me—pushed from the bus with a stout thrust—had one leg in the air while the dhoti of his other leg was hanging from my briefcase's handle. The back of my chicken friend's kurta was in shreds, but he had no idea. Then I discovered another nasty surprise. The stitching of my shoulder had been ripped apart, and my shirt's shoulder was hanging down my back.

Alongside the street where the bus stopped, there was a pharmacy bearing the name of some Dr Ansari. The signboard announced degrees such as AAUP, PMP and MD. The last brought a smile to my face—so what of those who claimed that once doctors got advanced degrees, they never left the city! But when I looked again at the signboard, after the MD, there were parentheses in which was written in Urdu—I mean, Farsi—'Managing Director, Ansari Clinic'. This is what MD meant. Now I wanted to discover the real meanings of AAUP and PMP! PMP was easy to guess: *private medical professional*. But I would have to wait a day to figure out the meaning of AAUP.

In the pharmacy, there was a yawning octogenarian and a thousand flies. In front of the store, there were two takhts where a half dozen people were talking while stretched out in various yogic positions, though not one from which a person could quickly get up. As far as conversation went, only one person was speaking, and the others were noisily listening.

2. Iqbal Mian

My friend was a teacher. I didn't know where he lived.
I stopped to ask.

I interrupted a conversation about India's misery. As
should be the case, no person, especially no person such
as myself, should be prioritized ahead of the country.
'. . . you say politicians have ruined the country. That's
entirely wrong! The whole country is in the hands of the
bureaucracy! It's a kingdom of bureaucrats! Whatever the
bureaucrat wants, that's what happens!'

There was nothing new to this argument, but I might
have unwittingly nodded my head in agreement. In
reaction to this, the speaker stared at me with wide eyes, as
though to confirm that if I wasn't a wasp, and that though
I wasn't local, I was nevertheless human. He said, 'Look at
what happened this 26 January. Look at the miracle that
some bureaucrat managed. 26 January is a holiday. But this
loser moved it and put it on Sunday. One day of holiday for
the poor was wiped out!'

It was a subtle point. People tried hard to understand.
Then he said, 'Even the ministers had no idea.'

One man opened his mouth, paused, then decided to go
ahead with his comment, 'But, Iqbal Sahib, which date falls
on what day is hardly the work of any bureaucrat or minister.'

'Then who decides?' he said, looking in my direction
for approval. His audience was silent.

I asked for my friend's address.

The speaker was around sixty years old. He wore a kurta
and tehmad around his stout frame. He wore a square cap.

He had a big black mole on one side of his nose that, sitting beneath his big eyes, had taken hold of his entire face, like a ship of bloodthirsty pirates. The impression was that if he would shut his eyes halfway, his countenance would be even more inscrutable, which would definitely give an added 'umpf' to religious speeches.

3. What My Friend Said

'It's great you met Iqbal Sahib as soon as you got here. He's the richest man in town. He's pretty smart too. In the last election, he was on the ruling party's ballot. He almost won.'

'He proved that from the start. He said that a Delhi bureaucrat in some office establishes which date falls on what day.'

My friend raised an eyebrow, thought for a second, then said, 'So, tell me, who *does* decide that?'

I couldn't believe his response, but quickly I offered an answer, 'All of this is done by Mr Ganeshan.'

'Which Mr Ganeshan?'

'You didn't read the papers? The one who just married his widow's sister.'

It was always like that with us. The two of us laughed loudly, as though I had just pulled ahead in our ongoing contest of wit.

'Actually, Iqbal Mian is a type of specialist. Outside his specialty, he doesn't know anything.'

My friend's place was on the second floor of the building next to the road. He had two small rooms. On the far side of the roof, there was a small room for his kitchen. Then, in the other direction, there was a place to bathe—an open-air room surrounded by walls. This second room also had something astonishing: a clean toilet. He must have used a very good bucket for flushing. In the bathing section, there was a hand pump, but you had to be careful with the handle because it rubbed against the rough wall.

Using the hand pump, I tore the skin on my fingers against the wall. I put some Dettol antiseptic cream on the wound, then went to stand outside the kitchen, where I felt the tingly effects of the medicine on my skin. My friend was lighting the stove to make tea, and he picked up the thread of his hagiography of Iqbal: 'With specialists, it's often like that. Look at yourself. You're an expert on village economy. If you were asked about some physics problem, you'd be at a loss. Just like Iqbal Mian, right?'

'Yes, but what's Iqbal Mian specialty?'

'He too, you could say, is a specialist of village economics. In particular, there's no one that can touch his knowledge about the cutting down of trees and the uses of forest timber.'

'You mean the protection of the environment and forestry?'

'If you mean stealing and robbing, then yes.'

In order to get from the street to my friend's place, you had to walk down a two-and-a-half-foot wide alley to get to the backyard where there was a set of stairs. This narrow, steep staircase was like a ladder to heaven. You had to ascend, holding onto a greasy rope secured to the wall. One misstep and you would go straight to heaven.

My friend's conversation made me feel like someone had grabbed me by the throat and tossed me down the stairs, all the way to the ground.

4. Chewing Tobacco and Computer Training

In just one day, I learned a lot about the story of the village's development. It was the Block Development Officer—whom everyone called the B.D.O. Sahib—who explained things to me. And it was he who broke down the mystery of the AAUP in Dr Ansari's title: it meant 'allopathic, ayurvedic, yunani physician'.

The B.D.O. Sahib was my friend's friend. We met one evening. He was very tired, but his face showed the satisfaction of having accomplished important work. He refused any and all food or beverages—tea, coffee, liquor, even a meal. He lay down and relaxed on a charpoy, then took out his own suckable snack, meaning, chewing tobacco. From a little metal box, he took out lime slake and mixed it with tobacco. On the palm of his left hand, he rubbed the lime slake and the chewing tobacco together, then he slapped it repeatedly, got rid of the stray bits, then placed it between his teeth and lower lip. He said, 'This evening was the last of the computer training. Somehow it finally wrapped up. My honor is safe!'

I hadn't seen anyone mix chewing tobacco in this backward way in a long time. To see this from someone mentioning computers was even stranger. I asked, 'In this town?'

He got up, spit out his tobacco juice, then went on talking, 'Tomorrow I have to show the officers-in-training some development work in the area, and then the forest. All of them will meet the forest officers. They sent their men 150 kilometres away to get pastries and fried cashews. You'll come tomorrow, too, won't you?'

'Computer training? In this town?'

'This isn't a town, sir, it's a village. We've just over 4000 people. Once we talked about consolidating with other villages to make a town, but all the villagers were opposed to it.'

'Why?'

'They didn't want to be taxed.'

'But the village is developing, right?'

'That happens by itself.'

Then, in one long breath, the B.D.O. Sahib started talking about tantric practices, astrology, archaeology, meteorology, sociology, novels and poetry. He started in on stories about the local development projects in the forest region affecting the thirty or thirty-five villages where he had family members— schemes that in the language of the Planning Commission bore the titles of 'self-generating', 'self-propagating', 'infrastructure', 'orchestration' and 'take-off stage'.

I, the well-known eccentric journalist (and in the friendly language of my friend, the 'specialist of village economy'), was all ears.

5. The Voice Louder Than All Others

Over the last twenty years, the development of the little forest village of Umraonagar had happened by itself. That's why the village was chosen out of all regional villages for intensive development. The person who had chosen the village was in fact the regional state representative.

Exactly two years before, the representative had been elected to the state assembly. And just as any story must advance past the beginning, he too tried to advance. To the Transportation Ministry. His cut was eight anna for every bus that went to Umraonagar. Once he became a representative in the state legislature, his cut increased to all of the profits. Verma Sahib, who was the head of the local transportation union, as well as Thekedar Sahib, the construction boss, and Thakur Sahib, the wealthy landlord, as well as other principal players, raised a ruckus that the man was set to become the state's transportation minister. More critique was published in the papers. But no one could anticipate the actions of the state's chief minister, and this representative became instead the State Minister of Sugar Factories. In any event, Umraonagar's transportation union welcomed him eagerly, and the newspapers described in rosy superlatives how the welcome event was 'splendid' and how the speeches were 'magnificent'. He also announced at the event that he would open up a cooperative sugar mill in Umraonagar.

A hand mill for grinding flour and a sugar mill capable of processing 2000 metric tons of cane are two different things. The ministry's more cautious officers tried to explain this to him. For a hand mill, all you have to do is run some electrical wire to the nearest pole. But you need more than that for sugar. At the very least, you need sugarcane. Umraonagar was completely surrounded by protected forest. The sugarcane would have to be brought in from far away, and even that amount would not be enough. The issues were explained in brief. But he became stubborn. Like every other minister, he already knew everything about bureaucracy, and so he could call good advice bad and bad advice good. In the end, he kept repeating his intentions. While he was repeating himself, the state's chief minister heard a voice from deep within his mind call out to him (in other words, he heard the ultimatum drawn up from his party's high command), and he resigned without any forewarning, as often happens these days. In the new administration, the local politician, unfireable by virtue of being his community's lone representative, went back to being a representative in the state legislature. Nevertheless, it was still not clear to the transportation union members what exactly his job was. That is, he was a state representative of the Department of Administrative Reform and Public Grievances.

The second event was also called 'splendid' and 'magnificent', but it wasn't as good. Imagine if the shopkeepers went all out in decorating their shops, but no one could tell what they sold—that was how to describe the minister, as well. People didn't understand what 'administrative reform' and 'public grievance' meant. But the minister was no less energetic. This time he made a new announcement: 'Following the leadership of our great prime minister, we will have to develop new forms of technology and new forms of knowledge. For example, all children should learn about computers. Our top officials will be in charge of this initiative. And so we're planning a two-week training course to teach our senior administrators. It will be held in Umraonagar.'

Now tie-wearing, briefcase-totting officials who used to pass gas in air-conditioned Delhi offices were walking the alleys of Umraonagar with computers in tow.

The B.D.O. Sahib was relating all this to me while, like in documentaries made by the government's Film Division, noises behind him acted as the soundtrack. Below on the street, there was the heeing and hawing of grazing donkeys, the cacophony of truck horns, the sound of flour hand mills whirring, the sound of transistor radios playing in several stores simultaneously and, from another store, amplified to top volume, a folk tune that was almost obscene. A little while before this aural background was audible, the call to prayer had drowned everything out with its echo-heavy loudspeaker. The azan's glory lasts only several minutes. Then the devotionals from Swami Raghubardas's ashram swamped out all other sounds.

In the devotionals, both male and female voices could be heard, but the strongest voice was a female's. As the B.D.O. Sahib was finishing his anecdote, this female voice rose higher and higher into the very highest octave of her voice and never retreated. Then, the voice rose by one more note and went into an alap: *kiiii—ii—ii—ii, kiiii—ii—ii—ii*. It sounded like someone had burst a lung while shouting.

My brow must have furrowed. The B.D.O. Sahib said, 'Sounds like Siyadulariji has had a fit again!'

More on Siyadulariji later, after I tell you about the five houses. But, first, let's take a look back at the area in its earliest, darkest days.

6. Before Medicine

Just off in the distance, a dried-out but thick branch rose from the stump of a mango tree. It stretched toward the heavens, as though in supplication. Nearby, there was a house. It was Umraonagar's first proper house. Based upon the tree stump, you can guess, and would correctly guess, that this was once a mango orchard. The trees set back from the road were the first to get cut for the townspeople's stoves and fires. The trees along the road were the government's. And so, through a method of cutting them up without cutting them down, these trees were turned into stumps.

And this method? It was just like taxing without an actual tax. For example, several months ago, the price of petroleum products jolted up. People raised a hue and cry, so the government economists explained, 'Now, people, just think of it like this—it's not a price increase, it's like we put a tax on it.' The people who had to pay this tax raised a hue and cry again, so the economists explained again, 'We don't want to raise the tax rate, and we don't want to put a new tax on fuel. So, you see, we've raised the price!'

The villagers took the government's lead. Due to a lack of firewood, a husband would say to his wife, 'I'm going to cut some wood from the tree along the road.' All the branches were cut off, and only the freshest shoots remained. Then, the trunk was attacked. First, the bark was stripped. Then, the trunk was penetrated to extract bits of wood. And this went on. Afterwards, all that was left was a misshapen trunk and one branch, like an arm reaching up to the heavens. In the end—meaning, the tree's end—there was only a leafless withered skeleton. The tree's shape was ruined without the use of power tools, and, to sum things up, it looked like the oval of India on the map. In this way, the tree was all cut up without being cut down, and the number painted in tar onto the tree by the government would stay forever!

These skeletons lined the road for quite a way into the distance. As for the trees of the mango orchard that lay behind these skeletons, there was no need for such decorum. That was because they had already been laid to waste. That's where the house now used for the government dispensary was built.

Before this house was built, Umraonagar was a very backward village. It was said to be an administrative seat in Raja Umraosingh's kingdom. That is, the ziledar lived there. The raja had had some buildings built along both sides of the road for the ziledar and his administrative team. These were mud houses with tile roofs. Only the ziledar had a house with brick walls. Each house had a front verandah, and two walled-off spaces inside, which, if they had had windows, could have been called rooms. In their interior darkness, spiders, mosquitos, lizards, millipedes and scorpions took shelter by the dozens (and snakes too). The sun's rays, the winter wind, the summer wind and dust storms never penetrated these chambers. Each building also had a narrow verandah and courtyard inside. Between the buildings, there was a two-and-half-foot-wide path, which is to say that this civilization didn't lack proper architecture. Yet, they did lack the sewers of the Mohenjodaro Civilization. Not one building had plumbing. The raja knew that whatever was true about his country was also true of its water. Water always finds its own level.

What can be said for certain is that at the end of the era of the zamindars a lot of things were wiped away by the water and the lack of upkeep of these buildings. On their ruins, new houses were built. Some have been fortunate enough to be spared by the water. They have been saved. But dozens of people are involved in litigation centered on these houses. Each person claims that they bought the house from the Ziledar Sahib, and that they have the paperwork to prove it.

7. First House

The ziledar was a high-ranking officer. He earned twenty rupees a month. He lived there. Or not really 'lived', but he came for a couple nights a month to spend time with a boatman's daughter.

The buildings with tile roofs, which could have been used for shops, lined the road for about a hundred metres. Behind them, there were the big stands of mango and rosewood trees. And behind them, it was fields, the river and the forests. Beyond that, it was thick and impassable forests.

The climate inspired thoughts of romance. The only thing missing was people to put the romance into practice. For the most part, the tile-roofed houses and shops stood empty. Everyone was scared of getting robbed. Some of the tile-roofed houses were the ziledar's. He lived in one.

The boatman's widow and her parents lived in another, and the families of the boatman's brother and sister lived in another. The boatman's parents could have lived in one too, but they didn't. Their son had died very young. They thought their daughter-in-law was a bitch, but her parents thought she was a goddess. They also thought highly of the ziledar. They thought he was very kind and noble-spirited. This was what most people thought.

A couple of land managers lived in the other buildings. They lived alone. With the help of tharra liquor, distilled on the boatmen's property near the river, and with the help of the loving affection of other people's daughters-in-law and daughters, they lived a pleasant life. They weren't scared of being robbed. The robbers were their men.

As the time of the zamindars was nearing its conclusion, the landlords started selling their property. Some sold their wastelands and every last blade of grass and moved to the city, where they became members of the zila council, or, if they couldn't manage that, they became politicians in one party or another and started to remake their lives. Raja Umraosingh's children became ambassadors in various countries, and their on-site managers started racking their brains about how to sell off Umraonagar's fields, forests and state properties. Everything was for sale. But there were no buyers. Then, one disreputable but well-known family member of the king stepped in to help.

He was the leader of the zila cooperative union. He rented out five of Umraonagar's market buildings at a rate of six rupees per house per month. In these buildings, he opened up stores that sold cheap grain, sugar, clothes, kerosene and cement. And so, in six months, he bought three stores. But enough about him. We were talking about the village's first house.

The cooperative union shops did good business. It was only the cement that didn't do well. Perhaps it was in order to increase cement sales that the construction of the first house took two years. It was the cooperative union supervisor's house. After it was built, his opponents started crying corruption. In those days, corruption was still seen in a negative light. So, the leader claimed health concerns and retired from public life. The zila cooperative union then passed into many other people's hands. But the house stayed in the hands of the selfsame former supervisor.

8. Ram Is God, or Robbery

Bhagvan Rajneesh, Satya Sai Baba, Maharishi Yogi, Swami Sadachari. These and other men are the fruits of a scientific and technological age. Swami Raghubardasji is another link in this chain. The rumbling of his jet hasn't yet been heard on the international stage, but from the speed at which he rose into the Umraonagar sky, it seemed as though he had been transformed from a man into a god and from a god into a jet plane.

It was said that before becoming a god he was a principal at various girls' schools. The 'Enlightened One' didn't care about the intellectual beauty of his staff members, but he did care about their physical beauty, especially their facial beauty. Due to conflicts of body and mind, he suffered a lot there—I mean, at the girls' schools.

On average, once a year, he would be physically attacked and, every two or three years, transferred. This happened year after year. In the end, he figured things out, which was perhaps due to the barrel of a country-made pistol held in the strong hand of one girl's brother, who started following him even in his dreams. Or perhaps it was due to repeating the hagiography of Tulsidas or Vilamangala, or some other bogus prophet, in which the beautiful girl's every charm is torn away to reveal that she too is just blood and guts. Anyway, in this particular case, transferring him was no longer necessary. He resigned. For two years, he lived in a Himalayan cave, meditating and learning from a guru. Then, back in Umraonagar, he smeared the yellow paste of renunciation on his forehead and became a god. His religious order was up and running in no time. They had their own flag, they had their own costume (a yellow kurta and a yellow lungi for the men, and a yellow sari and a red blouse for the lady disciples—which suited some of them quite well), their own way of praying, their own path to enlightenment, their own prayer music (both bhajan and kirtan). They had everything: their own ashram, their own tradition of charity and even their own community kitchen.

What you have to understand is that Swami Raghubardas was an incarnation of Lord Ram. A girl named Siyadulari was selected to sit next to him on the throne. Her real name was Phulmati. She was the fruit of the ziledar's love for the fisherman's widow. The ziledar had also made sure she completed high school. Now, she was suddenly known as Siyadulari.

She had been singing devotionals at the top of her lungs for several days. Since there was no scope for her to sing stories from the Ramayana, Raghubardas had not yet let her go into the forest.

It was part of the customs of Umraonagar that, in the evening, right after the azan ended, the bhajans and the kirtans would start up. Calling this 'communal harmony' and 'unity in diversity', politicians pushed forward the example of the village. Communal violence could break out at any moment. But it hadn't. Why? Each side was still busy counting its own money, and it was their good luck that they hadn't yet achieved the status of being able to waste it.

9. The Second, Third, Fourth and Fifth Houses

Every Indian knows that their country is a country of traditions. Some foreigner said that a 'great being' leaves his footprint in the sands of time. But how long can this footprint last? Wherever the 'great being' of the nation emerges, that's where his 'eternal path' will be. So, to make a permanent mark in such a backwater, a 'great being' will have to thrust his neck forward, like a camel, to get noticed.

This is what the former leader of the cooperative union did. After resigning, he handed over power to the other members, but he kept the house for himself. This became a steadfast tradition. The directorship changed hands every two years, and, in that time, the new director would build himself a new house before stepping down. In ten years, five houses were built. It's lucky that after the fifth director, the government got rid of the board of directors and made a young official its administrator. If not, today in Umraonagar three-storeyed houses would still be sprouting up like bamboo scaffolding. Still, the hope was that the young official wouldn't break from tradition entirely, and it is said that, in this and that city, he has had several small bungalows built for himself. If traditions change slightly with the times and the tastes of individuals, then so be it. This is the meaning of social progress. If money earmarked for development only went to villages, and the cities were left untouched, then there would be an imbalance in developmental activities. So, we should regard the administrator as an unmatched coordinator of modernity and tradition who, in upholding the tradition of development, brought construction projects to modern cities, as he saw fit.

In any event, it was the houses that the former directors of the cooperative union had built that made Umraonagar a proper town. With houses come business. In the name of his dearly departed father, the first director leased the first floor of his house free of charge to a government dispensary. Both the local people and the government were more than surprised, and yet a dispensary opened up. On the opposite side of the street, a pharmacy opened. It stole the drugs from the dispensary to sell itself. It was the compounder's nephew's store. The nephew's name was Amjad Ansari, AAUP, PMP, etc. His medical practice was supported by the pharmacy, and his pharmacy was supported by the government dispensary.

Dr Ansari and the government doctor had no dispute. Actually, thanks to Dr Ansari, the government doctor was able to run the clinic while living in the city. The first of every month, he showed up right on time to collect his salary, a fourth of the cut from the compounder's private practice, and half of the proceeds that Dr Ansari earned from selling government drugs. Then he scurried back to the city.

Corruption was never mentioned in reference to second director's house. There was no question of giving it over—any floor of it—for the public good. In fact, through wringing as much rent from it as he could, the second director wanted to make clear that the house had been built from his own blood, sweat and tears, although he hadn't actually spent any money in its construction. He had a nephew who was a ranger in the Forestry Department. God knows through what influence and how exactly it came to happen, but, in only a couple of days, a branch office of the state Forestry Department opened up in the house. Not only that, but the backyard was also rented out. It became a state-level public park where, in no time at all, forest timber from the Forestry Department's branch office was used to put up a huge depot. But enough of that.

The third director pledged to open an even bigger office in his house than the Forestry Department branch office had. He also had several buildings in the city, which he leased to the post office. This was his speciality. He had connections in the postal service all the way up to Delhi. Yet, if he had opened a small post office branch in that village building in order to serve the needs of the people, the rent would still not have covered his monthly expenses for cashews and whisky, for which he had a strong and lasting love. So, he left the tried-and-true postal service and was forced to wander through the maze of endless half-functioning government branches. Finally, threats and bribes had their effect. In the house, a centre for officer training in village development and village self-upliftment was opened. Despite the fact that inside the house there were good toilets and bathrooms, outside, on the street, there was always a line of young men wearing T-shirts and lungis, holding their little tin pots for butt-washing. These were the young men who had come for officer training. Now, this was the same building being used for computer training for high-ranking officers.

The fourth house's owner was a little on the strange side. He opened a fish husbandry office in the building. Reproducing the loathsome pronunciation of the majority of Doordarshan newscasters, people called his underlings 'pissing' (for 'piscine') development officers. When some villagers filled in a puddle or a pond and started planting grain on the land, then the 'pissing' officers came, dug up the fields and started a fish husbandry scheme there.

The fifth house wasn't rented out. Its owner brought a bunch of things from the city in a broken-down truck and set up shop right there. He said, 'I'm staying here for good. I'm going to get creative.' And that's where he's stayed.

10. May Bad Fortune Strike Those Who Wish Us Evil

That truck was sold a year ago, and two more came in its place. Now, in front of the building, there are also two buses and a jeep. On the back of the trucks had been written all sorts of proverbs, bits of poetry and slogans like 'victory to the youth, victory to the farmers'. These words revealed each truck's personality or community. The only proverb they shared was 'May bad fortune strike those who wish us evil'. Beneath these words, a shoes were painted on each truck. This meant that the truck's owner was one and the same person. He was the fifth house's owner. With his business's growth, people had forgotten his original name, caste and tribe. Now, his name was simply Thakur Sahib. He owned all the buses and other vehicles too.

Even if the old truck was just as broken down as ever, it could still carry heavy loads of rosewood logs. So, Thakur Sahib (who used to be called Ramesar Bhai) started using it to carry rosewood logs. In one direction, the road went to the city and, in the other direction, it passed through the forest. It was very old. People said that in the Treta Yug, Ram, Lakshman and Janaki had walked on it. So, you can imagine how old the rosewood trees must have been. Their lumber was practically as heavy as iron. Thakur Sahib dedicated his broken-down truck to these trees. Every night, one tree or another was being cut down and its timber was being sent off to the city, while its leaves, twigs, branches and extras went on to some nearby village. This work went along without a hitch for several months because the road's junior engineer was at the time one of Thakur Sahib's old classmates. But Thakur Sahib didn't do this business for long. The seed capital that he earned in the city from selling this priceless timber was collected under the rubric of the developmental policies of national banks, and he slowly started putting together a fleet of trucks and buses. In the beginning, he had to give half of the revenue from one of the trucks to the junior engineer and half of the revenue of one of the buses to a state representative. When that politician became Minister of State, Thakur Sahib offered the bus in full to the nation, through the minister's auspices.

The need for development never ends. That's what the Planning Commission has said. Just think how much construction took place in the city with the rosewood timber shipped there! Just think how many new neighborhoods and houses were built! This could be written about, as well. But, please forgive me, I still have so much to say about Umraonagar.

Thakur Sahib was now an important man. He had diabetes and high blood pressure. Impotence would soon follow. But, day by day, his mustache grew, and it made him look more fierce than ever. He had become so rich that he no longer talked about his early days, and yet he never stopped telling the story of how his transportation union became so powerful in that area.

"'May bad fortune strike those who wish us evil" isn't just a saying,' Thakur Sahib was explaining to my teacher friend, mostly for my benefit. 'Master Sahib, I developed this persona to make people think twice before wishing me evil. Master Sahib, I've never done anything. You know better than anyone. Whatever outsiders think when they see my moustache, I'm really a peace-loving man. Let liars lie, but you know the truth! Think about what was here before my buses! Just Iqbal Mian's two ramshackle buses— and ikkas. And those ikkas? They could travel only twenty-five kilometres and then people would have to transfer to buses coming from Umariya. That was the only way to reach the cities. I spent hundreds of thousands of rupees on my buses, then Iqbal Mian brought in more buses, then Verma's buses started up. Now you can reach the city in two and half hours, no problem! People in Umariya used to drive tempos, but then our union spent hundreds of thousands on buses. So, I'm telling you, Master Sahib, could the tempos have lasted? No. But I didn't do anything to them. It was Iqbal Mian—he got to them. The tempo drivers put their tails between their legs and slunk back into their holes.'

'And there used to be government buses,' I interjected.

'Okay, good for them. We didn't stop them from running. It was schoolboys. I heard there was a rude bus driver. He was beaten up somewhere. And the buses stopped running. You think I could have stopped them from running? Please. The government drivers don't want to drive this route. Are you stirring up rumors to give my buses a bad name?'

'What I'm thinking is that you should shave off your mustache,' my teacher friend said. 'Silly people say things about you.'

I told him not to shave it off, and I explained the importance of having a big moustache. He was reassured.

Then my teacher friend spoke in a half-teasing and half-provoking way, 'But, Thakur Sahib, you had the daily rail service shut down.'

He laughed at this, 'I know, I know. It was thanks to Iqbal Mian. The outbound train from the city stopped here in the morning, then stopped in the evening on the way back. But then it was cancelled. People were flying off the handle saying Iqbal Mian had greased the palms of the people in charge of the rail schedule. I had my suspicions, too. But, I swear to god, our union didn't fork out one single penny! The railway was losing ground. Then it was cancelled. That's all I know.'

I walked to the station the next morning at dawn. It was a romantic place. Thick forests surrounded it. Birds were everywhere. There wasn't anyone there at all. There was a night train that went to the city. It stopped at two in the morning. The train coming from the city stopped at three in the morning. The rail authorities were presently changing the station from a fixed stop to a flag station. If there had been any threat to the friendship of people, goats and chickens travelling together on the buses, it was long since a thing of the past.

11. The Story of Religion's Role in Development

It was no ordinary work to chop down rosewood trees for four or five hours in the middle of the night, leaving a wasteland behind. It required a tightly run ship, like at the circus where, as soon as the lion has leapt through the hoop, it takes just the blink of an eye for the circus workers to set the stage for a man to be shot out of the cannon. And Thakur Sahib had put in place such an organization. With the expansion of his transportation business, his powers had grown in other ways, as well. His activities were the catalytic converter for Umraonagar's development.

He had eight lead workers. Out of these, one got drunk and was crushed by his own truck. Then, a union leader sacrificed another worker in the coal mines of Bihar. Nothing so graphic happened to the remaining six. Some tip-top shops were built for them on the road leading from town. The tile-roof buildings were torn down, and, with the seed capital from the sale of the rosewood trees, the shops were set up to sell everything—from Ayurvedic remedies for impotence to diesel engine pumping equipment. Then, there, in the park, the Ram–Janaki temple was built with the same funds. The bank down the road from the temple was, as well. Banks should have opened in Umraonagar, especially when it seems these days like bank branches are opening everywhere, even on the back of a mule grazing in a field. Thakur Sahib took out loans from banks in order to build this one bank. But it was said that he lent this loan money at an interest rate three times of what a real bank charged, since the type of work for which he loaned money was the type of work that banks shied away from. He had found a market where others feared to go.

The town developed through religious rivalries. What happened was Iqbal Sahib paid for a mosque to be built in some empty land, then across from it in other some empty land a Hindu temple's foundation was laid. The mosque was never completed. The expensive tiles that were to go on top of the minaret's whitewashed red bricks were never sent from Hyderabad. But, no matter, loudspeakers with an amplifier were installed. At the same time, Swami Raghubardas's ashram grew up next to the temple. In fact, it spread over some of Iqbal Mian's land. Call it 'communal harmony' or 'unity in diversity', or say it was due to Thakur Sahib's strong-arm tactics, but Iqbal Mian ceded the land to the ashram.

During this time, Lord Ram, alias Swami Raghubardas, was ensconced on his throne. He didn't look anything like Ram's avatars. Not like Ajanbahu, Vrishskandh, Vyudhorask or Koti Manoj Lajavan. Under his heavenly halo, he looked like the oppressed, mediocre, tired-out country college principal that he had been.

Underneath a red velvet canopy decorated with strings of sparkling silver stars, the Raghuvanshi court announced its glory while Raghubardas and Siyadulari sat together on the throne. Lord Ram had noticed her when the Ziledar Sahib had sent her to study in his high school. Siyadulari sat as motionless as a statue, and her big, doe-like eyes were the only things on her dark and attractive face that moved.

Lord Ram recited a sloka, then started singing a bhajan that he had come up with himself. His worshippers were sitting in front of him, mostly girl devotees, and they quickly picked up the melody. Then, from another direction, the azan started to rumble through the loudspeakers.

The B.D.O. Sahib said, 'Up till now, everything has been fine. Thakur Sahib and Iqbal Mian get along pretty well. Only once or twice have things almost got out of hand. I just heard they asked the police captain to station an armed police brigade in the area. The upper floors of Thakur Sahib's house are empty. He wants to go live in a smaller house. He's ready to rent out the house to the brigade. And the arrangements for the police commander will be made by Iqbal Mian.'

12. Mazhar Mian's Religious Processional

Thakur Sahib and Iqbal Mian's mutual understanding was based on a principle of the moral code that neighboring kingdoms should respect each other's borders. In the forests around Umraonagar, cutting down trees through hardworking though nefarious means was a long tradition. Iqbal Mian had a monopoly over the illegal lumber business. He used to live in a nearby village that was even smaller than Umraonagar. When electricity came to the area, he set up a power saw along the road to cut wood. Then it grew into a factory, and, with its proceeds, he built himself a house. From out of the government reserve, he cut out a little swath for himself. With his lot staked out, his younger brother Mazhar Mian started to help out.

Thakur Sahib never so much as looked at the government forest. That was Iqbal Mian's domain. His business was limited to the rosewood along the road. And so, though both were in the lumber business, they never so much as had a cross word for each other. Then, their friendship grew yet stronger when they met in the transportation union.

At first, Mazhar Mian devoutly cut down the government forest and sent the trees to his brother's factory. When he took up residence in the second house, he set up a branch of the Forestry Department and thus found his life's true calling. The first year after the branch was established, he sold timber at auction at the highest prices in the entire state. That is, he sold to his brother Iqbal Mian. This branch started adding so much money to the state's till that the higher-ups in the Forestry Department started chirping and grunting like a bunch of wildlife. Being a branch manager in Umraonagar became a prestigious job. Each time a new manager was assigned, right after the first auction, his office would be flooded with congratulatory letters from top officials, and, based upon the Forestry Department's programme of both encouraging hardworking officers and demoting officers that slacked, an announcement would follow stating how the new branch manager was being awarded a prize, promoted and given a quick transfer. So, for the worst sort of corrupt officer, the job at Umraonagar became a guarantee of promotion. All of this was due to the generous heart of Iqbal Mian, alias Thekedar Sahib. The reason for this generosity is another matter altogether.

Where along the road there had been the shops of Thakur Sahib's friends, now there were a handful of timber, door, window and takht factories. These were owned by Iqbal Mian's men. Their primary business was revitalization. No, they weren't beauty parlors. I mean, they took in illegal wood and revitalized it to look like wood bought at auction. How? At the factory, timber was transformed into planks, platforms, doors, windows and so on. When it was loaded on a truck, it was impossible to know which wood was stolen and which was bought at the government auction, just like it's impossible to recognize stale horse fodder in ground coriander. You could stop and inspect timber before it was loaded onto a truck, but, after the product was made, it was impossible to know what was what.

That's why Iqbal Mian bought the government timber at auction at whatever price. He needed it at any price.

When the timber got to his factories, it turned into what industrialists, when they take on a loan, call 'margin money'. This is the way that he was able to pass off his inferior black market wood (of which he had nine times as much) as good wood and sell it at a much higher price. This was the method he used to establish his business 'Messieurs Iqbal Hussain and Brothers, Government Contractor and Timber Merchant'. As soon as the forestry officials started congratulating themselves upon his last exorbitant bid, his agents started cutting down more of the forest and sending it to his factories. As the profits grew, so too did the Forestry Department's moral decline. The good thing was that with a booming economy, you look at the profit graphs and never turn around to think about the long-term consequences.

13. Robbery, or National Development

The alley leading to my friend's house was so narrow that if a man and a woman happened to exit the alley at the same time, they would likely be charged with adultery, or the man with rape. At the time, there was trash and mud everywhere. My friend weaved his way through the obstacles, just a single electrical wire snaking along, then leapt over a wall onto the street. I followed. We were going to a party hosted by Iqbal Mian, alias Thekedar Sahib, a.k.a. the local representative from the Satta Party. We hadn't been initially invited, but then we got an invitation through the state finance minister.

The occasion was the end of the computer-training programme. The finance minister had come to give a speech to mark its conclusion. The occasion's main guest was the State Minister of the Department of Administrative Reform and Something Something Something. The B.D.O. Sahib was the MC. The location was the backyard of the third house. Dishes to be served were goat, chicken and fish. Entertainment was to be folk songs and Bhojpuri songs. The Bhojpuri song would narrate the legend of the 20-Point Programme and Rajiv Bhaiya's long-standing love for the poor and oppressed.

Some indigenous peoples still lived along the forest's edge. They supplied the goats and chickens. Over there, beyond a clump of trees, there was a piddly little river and some fishermen's houses. That's where they got their fish. Goats, chicken and fish were abundant in that area, as well as moonshine that was brewed along the river. And if you bought chickens or goats, you could get liquor at a discount. So, to summarize, food and drink was to be had, as long as you could pay, which Iqbal Mian could.

The finance minister was famous for believing that the Indian press was irresponsible and petty. But operating through the principle of not hating the messenger of bad news, he loved journalists. He treated executive editors and reporters to the best that his hospitality could offer. Managing editors and desk reporters were left with the dregs.

Even though I was technically part of the latter group, the finance minister knew me. So, my friend and I were included on the revised and final guest list. At the banquet, though I was the only reporter not tied to the government, I wasn't cast aside. The radiant light of the minister's smile kept finding its way to me.

After the banquet and the folk entertainment, and before the minister left, we had the chance to catch up. Even then, he talked only about national development, the poverty line, village uplift and so on. The finance minister mentioned the exceptional development of Umraonagar, asked if I didn't find it so, and said that the irrigation project that had been stalled for years due to the inability to procure the needed land was now all but ready to go forward.

'Then a market too will come about in short order?' I asked.

'Of course, it will. There will be so many workers coming to the area that they won't be able to work without a big, modern shopping area.'

Two or three days before, I had seen this particular marketplace. There were half-built buildings. Brick walls had moss growing on them. It was hard to say whether they were the ruins of old buildings or the beginnings of new buildings since the irrigation project had ground to a halt four years earlier. With the project's cement, metal and sundry leftover building materials, a man named Guptaji who owned a brick kiln had built as many buildings for the marketplace as possible. But, just like the irrigation project, the bazaar had gone belly up.

'You've only been here for a couple days. You've seen for yourself the rapid development of the area. Look here, the newspapers publish stories about murder, rape, highway robbery and so on. Shouldn't they write about places like here? I know you're interested in village economics. You'll write something, then?' the finance minister asked.

He and his cronies waited enthusiastically for my response. There was nothing for me to think about, but I acted like I was thinking. Then I gathered my breath, saw that Iqbal Mian, Thakur Sahib and some others were listening, and I addressed the minister in English: 'Of course, I would love to, but there's one point that I just can't reconcile. The national government and your finance ministry are always announcing a new war on the double economy, black money, tax evasion, embezzlement, fraud and so on. But after having studied a little about how things work here, I can say that if the government worked hand in hand with these other players, then development could happen very rapidly here. Yet, if stealing and skimming didn't take place in public works projects, then I'm convinced that despite a handful of government agencies having opened branches here, it would still be a thatched-roof village, and the healthy middle class of today would be living under the poverty line. These houses, these factories, these busy stores . . .'

Thakur Sahib interrupted. He said something that made me shut up.

'Are you calling all of us thieves and robbers?' he asked in English.

I spoke to him with all the courtesy I had left in me. To cool him down, I couched what I had to say in complicated economic terms so that he would understand that it hadn't been an insult but a theoretical analysis. I apologized for my part in the misunderstanding, and said, 'Not at all. I'm talking about something else. Take Delhi, for instance. Look at the last Asian Games. Millions and millions of rupees were spent to modernize the capital. In this, thousands of people of no consequence rose above the poverty line and left their low-class status behind. This was through nothing else but sheer robbery. They rose into the middle class by hiding money in their houses, their bank lockers and in the trunks of their cars. I'm convinced that if there wasn't such energy invested in this robbery and stealing, then there would be a huge cash windfall for you to use in your welfare schemes. But that takes time. It's also not clear whether what in the government's view is good for their welfare is, in their opinion, good for their welfare.'

The finance minster replied, 'You're a good joker, but even when making your jokes don't forget that 37 per cent of Indians live under the poverty line, and they place no trust in stealing and robbery.'

I replied, 'They will in time. From Umraonagar to New Delhi, the way the middle class steals as a side effect of national development isn't lost on the poor. Do the fishermen living here on the riverbanks not know that the bribe that the village development officer gets for giving loans for their fishing business can make him rich in just a year?' Then I spoke to the minister with a coaxing tone, 'Please believe me. Bribes and trickery and underhanded business . . . instead of condemning them, if you worked *with* them, in just a couple days, a really cohesive campaign for village development could be put in place. Just think how quickly development would take place then!'

The minister laughed heartily, then said, 'Your jokes never end. You really want to build the nation through corruption and stealing?'

Then my friend spoke for the first and only time, 'No, sir, that's not it. My friend is trying to theorize the way that development is taking place, thanks to you all.'

14. Between Kumbhipaka and Astipatra

Going home, I wanted to escape being in close quarters with goats and chickens. My friends and I were standing on the street in the early morning, waiting for an ikka. While the transportation union had put an end to rail service, government buses, tempos, taxis and so on, they had let ikka drivers continue plying their trade. It's an old tradition, the fear of one day falling on tough times. And so, in the same way that people don't light their old thatch on fire, the transportation union didn't interfere in the little business that ikka drivers had available to them.

We didn't have to wait for long. It was still dark to see anything, but we heard the ikka's approach. My friend asked it to stop, yelling, 'Stop! Stop!' Then, we both ran after it. But it didn't stop.

My friend threatened the driver with a horrible insult, 'Stop, asshole, or else . . .' The 'or else' had an immediate effect. The ikka stopped.

My friend started to ask the driver about whether I could get a ride. The ikka driver said that the rider—one 'Lalli'—had the ikka for herself, and that it was impossible to seat anyone else. But then Lalli tersely instructed the ikka driver that he was to let me on, if only we would hurry.

We call an ikka like that a 'kharkhara'. They sound like an ox cart going down the road—'kharkhara kharakhara . . .'

If the ikkas had been made of solid wood and if in place of a horse there had been two oxen yoked together, then it would have been an ox cart. I mean, it could only comfortably seat two people. It's another matter that she had to sit cramped and hunched over before we introduced ourselves.

Our introduction came several kilometres into our journey when she raised her niqab. The heavens and the stars didn't drop from the sky, but I was startled to see who it was. The purdah-keeping Lalli wasn't a Muslim lady. In the dim light, I recognized her. It was Siyadulari.

'Siyadulari? Is it you?' I asked.

'My name is Phulmati,' she said in a voice reserved for public-speaking events.

She slowly managed to worm her way out of her burka. Then she carefully folded it and put it in a bag. She wasn't wearing a yellow sari and a red blouse. She was wearing a nylon print sari. The color hadn't entirely set, but the sari didn't look bad on her.

I had several questions in mind but couldn't get one out. She answered one without my asking, 'He's a disgusting person.'

In order to show her I understood, I nodded my head. She said, 'You're not from here. So I can tell you. In three kilometres, there will be an intersection. There's a bus from Umariya that stops there. I'm getting on the first one.'

'And I'm taking that one back as well.'

'Don't take that one. It stops everywhere. Take the next one.'

Then the ikka driver spoke, 'Please get off before the intersection, sir. What's the point of having anyone see you two together?'

'Why would it matter?'

'Thakur Sahib and Swamiji Maharaj's devotees will bother Master Sahib. They'll think it was because of you two that I fled.'

'You're fleeing?'

At first she didn't answer. The ikka driver spoke, 'Her dad in the city is sick. She doesn't have anyone else. Swamiji Maharaj didn't give her permission to go.'

'The Ziledar Sahib is still alive?'

It was a stupid question. But it was entirely natural for me to ask. Hearing the old stories about him and about how the Ziledar Sahib had taken up with a fisherman's widow, I felt like he was a legend and not a real man.

This upset Phulmati. 'If he's not living, you mean he's dead? Is that what you want?'

I lowered my head to express how sorry I was for having spoken in such a way. She calmed down, then said, 'A long time ago, my dad started living in the city. That's where I went to school. My mom stayed in Umraonagar. She was sick all the time. She used to have sharp pains in her stomach. Then dysentery. Fever. I don't know what all. I think my dad's caught the same thing.'

I had to say something, so I asked, 'So, you're going to look after your dad?'

Then it was the ikka driver's turn to get upset, 'She couldn't do anything but leave! Swamiji Maharaj was getting a second Siyadulari. You must have seen her, Babuji, a very white, bright-faced girl is always sitting in front of him. Swamiji has started to say that Siyadulari will never be beautiful.'

'So, why didn't Swamiji want her to go?'

'That's Swamiji. You must know how he is.'

I got off a little before the intersection. I asked, 'And if you meet one of Swamiji's students?'

'I'm not scared of that here. Rakesh Bhai is already here.'

'Rakesh Bhai?'

'The leader of the Youth Party—that Rakesh. You don't know him? He's a very important youth leader.'

The birds were beginning to sing, but there was nothing as radiant just then as Phulmati. I put my hand on the ikka to stop it. My curiosity was finally getting the better of me.

'So, you'll live with your dad and work with Rakesh Bhai?' I asked.

'I'll study and work. Rakesh Bhai says that I speak very well. There's going to be a youth camp in the mountains. Rakesh Bhai says I'll have to give a lecture on spiritualism there.'

'On what?'

'On spiritualism. The physical world is nothing, right?'

I said goodbye and let the ikka go. For a second, I thought I should tell her about the ways of this insubstantial physical world where a fisherman's widow can find refuge in a good man and yet die alone with her sickness untreated, and where her daughter falls prey to social ills even scarier than what the widow experienced. But there wasn't time, and there was no one to listen to me. But, even then, the night's conversation took on the shape of a question that rose into the sky: Once you see for yourself the system of stealing and thieving that goes by the name of development (and that is the middle class's heaven), where is Phulmati's place in that?

In the Puranas, Kumbhipaka is a hell full of blood and gore. Another hell is called Astipatra, where trees have swords for leaves and slash at you with every step you take, scarring your flesh. As dawn lit that autumn day, my mind started to worry for the girl heading to the intersection where Rakesh Bhai awaited her, the girl who had escaped Kumbhipaka just to wander into Astipatra. Whether development in Umraonagar took place on the finance minister's principles, or through Iqbal Mian's savoir-faire, it would not take away any of the power of these hell realms. Thinking about Phulmati, I thought about how these two means of development were, in Umraognar, falling hand in hand to hell.

Acknowledgments

Thanks go out to my editors at Penguin Random House India, Ananya Bhatia and Rea Mukherjee, for supporting this project and for their timely and valuable editorial assistance. Also to Sohini Biswas. Thanks as well to Donald Breckenridge and Jen Zoble for publishing excerpts from this book in *The Brooklyn Rail* (Brooklyn, New York).